A Manual for Assertiveness Trainers

SECOND EDITION

Volume II of
The Professional Edition
of
Your Perfect Right

Robert E. Alberti, Ph.D.
Michael L. Emmons, Ph.D.

Impact ✺ Publishers ™
POST OFFICE BOX 1094
SAN LUIS OBISPO, CALIFORNIA 93406

Editions
First Edition, 1986
Second Edition, 1990
Second Printing, October, 1991
Copyright © 1986, 1990
by Robert E. Alberti and Michael L. Emmons

Library of Congress Cataloging-in-Publication Data
Alberti, Robert E.
 A manual for assertiveness trainers / Robert E. Alberti, Michael L. Emmons. — 2nd ed.
 p. cm. — (The Professional edition of Your perfect right: v.2)
 Includes bibliographical references and index.
 ISBN 0-915166-70-4 (pbk. : alk. paper)
 1. Assertiveness training. I. Emmons, Michael L. II. Title.
III. Series: Alberti, Robert E.   Professional edition of Your perfect right: v. 2.
RC489.A77A53   1990 vol. 2
158'.2 a—dc20
[158'.28]   90-5326
                                                              CIP

Publisher's Note
This publication is designed to provide accurate and authoritative information in regard to the subject matter covered. It is sold with the understanding that the publisher is not engaged in rendering psychological, medical, or other professional services.

Printed in the United States of America on acid-free paper
Published by **Impact ✍ Publishers™**
POST OFFICE BOX 1094
SAN LUIS OBISPO, CALIFORNIA 93406

CONTENTS

INTRODUCTION

When we began *Your Perfect Right* in the summer of 1970, we had in mind a guide for counselors.

We were not even sure it should take the form of a book. After all, wasn't assertiveness training a very simple process of teaching skills? Why not just a few sheets of instructions so a trained counselor could conduct AT systematically? Fortunately, somewhere in the process of putting together that first edition, we recognized that the material would be more useful in book format, and that AT's "simplicity" is deceptive, and that there might even be a few non-counselor folk who would be interested. And the "guide for counselors" — as a separate volume — didn't come to pass for another sixteen years.

A "facilitator's section" in the second, third, and fourth editions was expanded and updated with the fifth edition in 1986, and introduced as this *Professional Edition of Your Perfect Right.* Now — twenty years and 900,000 copies after the idea — there exists a new edition of our original intent.

1

We have elected to separate the popular and professional sections of *Your Perfect Right* to better serve the interest of the vast majority of readers: about one-hundred-to-one copies are purchased by individuals interested in their own personal growth, rather than in training others. They want to help themselves. We decided it was time to unburden them from 128-or-so pages of trainer's manual.

The *Professional Edition* is presented in two volumes, with the popular *Your Perfect Right* included because so much of our approach to training is represented in that work. The chapters are numbered sequentially from those in the popular volume; thus this material begins with chapter 21.

This volume covers four general topic areas (although we have not divided it into formal "sections"): preparation of the trainer; preparation of the trainee; individual and group training procedures; applications of assertiveness training.

We have concentrated on a clear explication of our own procedures, and added material from the literature to provide a comprehensive picture of the field.

It is our hope that human service professionals and those in training will find this a useful resource. We would appreciate your feedback as an aid to improving future editions.

ON BECOMING A PROFESSIONAL TRAINER

Who is a "professional" assertiveness trainer? How does one prepare to become an assertiveness trainer?

Over the last two decades, we have conducted training workshops and seminars throughout the country to help answer those questions. The material in this volume has grown out of those seminars, our counseling and teaching, and the current research literature of the field. Designed both for professional facilitators and facilitators-in-training, this manual covers the information, skills and procedures required to help others develop effective assertiveness and other social skills.

Assertiveness, Self-Expression, Social Skills, or What?

Assertiveness training emerged out of the efforts of early behavior therapists to systematize effective procedures for behavioral treatment of anxiety, phobias, social inadequacy, and other symptomatic disorders. Salter (1949) described a process of coaching his clients in "excitatory" behavior, a technique very much like that which later became known as assertiveness training. Wolpe and Lazarus (1966) were first to use the term "assertive training," and laid much of the groundwork for the process. Our first edition of *Your Perfect Right* in 1970 was the first book solely devoted to AT, and the first detailed, step-by-step explication of the procedure.

During the 1970's AT became a popular fad, and a few dozen books and thousands of articles were published, aimed at both popular and professional audiences, along with hundreds of doctoral dissertations examining aspects of the field.

During this period, in an effort to distance themselves from the "pop" movement, and to stake a claim to territory broader than "assertiveness," a number of behavior therapists began to describe their work as "social skills training" (SST). In that context, a comment by L'Abate puts the topic in perspective:

> *From its early beginnings as "assertiveness training," the scope of this movement has expanded until now it must be considered one of the most widely deployed intervention strategies for the delivery of mental health services. (1985, p.xi).*

Although there are important differences in scope between   assertiveness training and social skills training — SST does cover a broader range of behaviors than those strictly considered "assertive" — we will use the terms interchangeably here. A very recent published report (Hollin and Trower, 1989) provides an updated review and critique of the social skills training literature.

Assertiveness and social skills training are now commonplace in graduate programs in counseling, social work, psychology, nursing, HRD, theology, management, and others (including a controversial procedure for classroom teachers called "assertive discipline"). Let us say for the record, *we do not universally endorse all approaches, methods, or procedures which use the term "assertive."*

In the material which follows, we have attempted to broaden the usual human service professional model to meet the needs of a variety of disciplines, since many readers of this material will not be trained in psychology or in psychological methodology.

Nevertheless, a caveat is in order.

Your work may be in business or government human resource development, in a paraprofessional role in a health or human services agency, in classroom teaching or coaching, in the allied health professions, in college student development, in pastoral counseling or a host of other fields outside psychotherapy. As a result, you may consider it unnecessary to increase your psychological sophistication before you conduct assertiveness training. Unfortunately, we're not going to let you off that easily!

The procedures of AT/SST are essentially psychological in nature, and *anyone* who offers this service, regardless of the context, should be familiar with the basic principles discussed or referred to here. While AT/SST procedures are deceptively simple, their skillful application demands careful preparation and sensitivity to a number of intrapersonal and interpersonal characteristics.

Qualifications of Facilitators

As a foundation for training others, potential assertiveness trainers should be effective in their own social and assertive skills, and should participate in assertiveness training as trainees.

Specific training is necessary if one is to become a *qualified* facilitator of social behavior in others. We consider it particularly important that professionals prepare themselves to offer a high level of service, since an unfortunately large amount of work called "assertiveness training" has been done by persons without adequate qualifications (including more than a few who have simply participated in an AT group and then undertaken to offer training to others).

The statement of *Principles for Ethical Practice of Assertive Behavior Training* (Appendix A) identifies general and specific qualifications for interventions at three levels: assertive behavior *training;* assertive behavior *therapy;* and *training of trainers.* We support and advocate the standards identified in that statement.

The "General Qualifications" section of the *Principles* identifies the following minimum requirements for professional facilitators in all settings and at all levels:

• Understanding of basic principles of learning and behavior;

• Understanding of anxiety and its effects upon behavior;

• Knowledge of limitations, contraindications, and potential dangers of social skills training;

• Training as a facilitator under qualified supervision.

Additional "Specific Qualifications" detailed in the statement suggest the need for graduate level training in one of the human services professions (e.g., psychology, education, social work, counseling, HRD, nursing, medicine, human development, pastoral counseling, public health). The level of training proposed increases as one assumes increasing responsibility: least formal training is required for those who would do non-clinical *training*; more for those who would do AT as *therapy*; and most for those who would *train trainers*.

The difference between training and therapy is not always clear, but the ethics statement offers quidelines to help facilitators decide if their qualifications are adequate (see 3.2.A, 3.2.B, and 5.A-G).

It is our hope that behavioral criteria for qualification of facilitators will make "academic" credentials less important. Dr. Pat Jakubowski of the University of Missouri developed a set of behavioral "competencies" for AT facilitators several years ago. We have seen no published version of her work, however. Adequate formal training and the other qualifications identified in this chapter and in the *Statement of Principles for Ethical Practice* remain the most adequate criteria available.

Additional Recommended Preparation
In addition to the specific recommendations in the ethics statement, we suggest that potential facilitators acquire the following preparation:

Knowledge of Basic Social Learning Principles. Professionals trained in psychology and counseling should have mastered this background in their academic preparation. Individuals in other fields should make special efforts to become familiar with the principles of social learning, including conditioning, reinforcement, extinction, behavior shaping, modeling, and cognitive restructuring. Familiarity with these principles is basic to all AT interventions, whether or not you employ a "behavioral" approach. Recommended resources are Bandura's (1969) *Principles of Behavior Modification*, Beck's (1976) *Cognitive Therapy and the Emotional Disorders*, and Wolpe's (1973) *Practice of Behavior Therapy*.

Familiarity with the Literature of AT. When the first edition of *Your Perfect Right* was published in 1970, we were able to present virtually the entire literature of the field in a bibliography of two-dozen items (including several which were not specifically AT references). By 1983, the fourth edition of a biennial *Annotated Bibliography of Assertiveness Training Literature* included nearly one-thousand items! No doubt even that impressive list was not totally inclusive of the field, since many papers have appeared in unexpected journals.

It is expected that professionals will remain up-to-date in their respective disciplines. In addition, we recommend attention to the material cited in the professional bibliography in this volume.

Special Training. Seminars, training courses, workshops, institutes, and graduate programs for trainers in assertiveness and social skills training are offered by a wide variety of professional associations, institutions and individuals, and should be investigated. Carefully assess the qualifications of the leaders of such programs according to the standards described in this chapter. Especially helpful in announcing further training for professionals are:

Association for Advancement of Behavior Therapy's *the Behavior Therapist* (420 Lexington Avenue, New York, NY 10170);

American Association for Counseling and Development's *Guidepost* (5203 Leesburg Pike, Falls Church, VA 22041);

American Psychological Association's *Monitor* (1200 Seventeenth Street, N.W., Washington, D.C. 20036).

Practice with Components. Actually experiencing the full range of the assertiveness training process in a variety of typical situations enables the facilitator more fully to understand what the client experiences. If a client is having difficulty expressing anger in a situation, you will be much more helpful if you have worked with similar situations as a trainee through covert rehearsal, modeling, roleplaying, shaping, and coaching. One approach is to practice with a staff colleague or a client volunteer. Get together and alternate the roles of client and facilitator, experiment with a variety of situations and techniques. Video tape equipment is invaluable in the learning process. If available, some type of physiological measuring and feedback device may also provide useful data.

Chapters 23, 24, and 25 of this manual present more detail on the training procedures with which you must become familiar. Also, please review Chapters 6, 9, 11, and 12 in *Your Perfect Right*.

Personal Effectiveness. Anyone who sets out to increase assertiveness or other social skills in others must first *be* actively assertive and socially competent. The passive knowledge of assertive behavior gained by reading this or any book is only a beginning. In our personal lives we are continually aware of situations in which these principles can be applied. This awareness has major benefits, including keeping the "air clear" in our own interpersonal functioning, and adding to our on-going examples to report to our clients and groups.

Commitment to Ethical Principles. Since AT/SST has become so popular in recent years, we are concerned about high standards of practice, and appropriate qualifications and ethics of facilitators. Evaluate your own qualifications in the light of the statement of *Principles for Ethical Practice of Assertive Behavior Training*, and offer only those services for which you are truly qualified. We urge you to become familiar with the statement and, if you are or intend to be an AT facilitator, to support and function within its guidelines.

A Self-Assessment Inventory for Facilitators

Originally a therapeutic procedure for counter-conditioning high levels of social anxiety, assertiveness training has become — as noted earlier — an integral part of the training and personal development processes of the fields of education, psychological therapy, nursing, management, personnel development, rehabilitation, social work, corrections.... As a result, the usual preparation of facilitators — supervised training in the methodology of psychological assessment and therapeutic intervention — does not apply to most AT leaders.

To give prospective facilitators of AT a personal guideline for assessing their own qualifications, we have prepared the following self-assessment inventory. Much of this material is derived from the statement of "Principles for Ethical Practice of Assertive Behavior Training."

We suggest you rank yourself on each item, honestly noting your own strength. Then seek to *develop* those skill/attitude/content areas on which you are weak *before you do assertiveness training!* Get special training, supervision, practice; do some research or extensive reading in the literature; attend professional training workshops or seminars. A simple evaluation procedure is to rate yourself on a four point scale: *4. Strong; 3. Adequate; 2. Need work; 1. Not sure.* Go to work on those which deserve only a *1* or *2*!

* * *

"BEFORE YOU DO ASSERTIVENESS TRAINING"
A Self-Assessment Inventory for Facilitators
Robert E. Alberti, Ph.D., and Michael L. Emmons, Ph.D.

A. How adequate is your background of training and experience to prepare you for the level of AT intervention you intend to employ? (TRAINERS should have strength on items 1-6 and 7 or 8 or 9; THERAPISTS on 1-6 and 7 or 8 or 9 and 10 and 11; TRAINERS OF TRAINERS on all.)

1. Principles of human learning and behavior   _____

2. Anxiety and its effects   _____

3. Fundamental principles of AT   _____

4. Limitations, contraindications, and potential
   dangers of AT   _____

5. Participation in AT as a client   _____

6. Supervised practice as an AT facilitator   _____

7. Certification for independent practice OR   _____

8. Agency sponsorship with supervision OR   _____

9. Direct supervision by a certified professional   _____

10. Clinical internship or supervised professional
    practice   _____

11. Advanced degree in a human services field   _____

12. Advanced study and practice in AT   _____

B. How well prepared are you to assess the *needs* and
readiness of your clients for assertiveness training?

1. Familiarity with psychological assessment
   principles   _____

2. Sensitivity to high levels of anxiety in clients _____

3. Ability to discern appropriateness of AT for client
   needs   _____

4. Awareness of attitudes, skills, obstacles affecting
   assertiveness   _____

5. Comfort in making referrals when necessary   _____

6. Awareness of client needs and limits holistically   _____

C. Do you maintain a *holistic* perspective in regard to the needs of your clients? More specifically, how effective are your procedures (direct or via referral) for:

1. Assessment and intervention for conditions
    other than assertive or social skills deficits (e.g.
    anxiety, psychopathology, antisocial aggression)   _____

2. Assessment/treatment/referral for client
    physical functioning   _____

3. Assessment/treatment/referral for client
    psychological functioning   _____

4. Assessment/treatment/referral for client
    spiritual functioning   _____

5. Assessment/treatment/referral for client
    social functioning   _____

6. Assessment/treatment/referral for client
    vocational functioning   _____

D. How firm is your commitment to responsible ethical practice of assertiveness training, including the areas noted below?

1. Client self-determination   _____

2. Ethical behavior of facilitator   _____

3. Appropriateness of intervention   _____

4. Social responsibility   _____

Self-Improvement for Facilitators

Any procedure which involves interventions in the lives of other persons must be performed carefully, and with adequate monitoring of the interventions to assure a high level of ethical and professional responsibility. The quality of human care is only as good as the qualifications of practitioners.

We suggest several specific activities trainers may undertake in order to monitor and enhance their own effectiveness:

• *Continuing professional education.* Even if it's not required in your profession, we hope you're regularly attending professional meetings, workshops and seminars to keep yourself up to date. Scan the professional literature — in print or on-line — and study carefully those reports which touch on your work. Spend time in the library, order from publishers' catalogs which come in the mail, or join book clubs to keep abreast of recent developments which find their way into print.

• *Client/trainee feedback forms.* Routinely requesting client/trainee feedback on your work will be of great help in determining the adequacy of your interventions. Individual client judgements are of limited value of course, but the patterns of responses from numbers of your trainees will show areas of strength and weakness in your presentations. Oral feedback can help too, of course, but won't be as critical or as detailed as that contained in anonymous written form.

• *Audio/videotapes of your sessions.* For facilitators as for clients, there is no better feedback device than to hear and see yourself "in action." At least several times a year, set up recording equipment to capture your own performance on tape — then watch and listen (preferably with help from a colleague).

• *Audio/videotapes of others' work.* Just as in your training, and with your clients, modeling is a powerful continuing education device. Watch your colleagues doing what you do, to get ideas, to refresh yourself, to keep abreast.

• *Peer review.* Invite your colleagues into your training sessions to view your work. Encourage them to critique you honestly, and listen to their comments. Videotape can be used effectively here too, of course.

• *Clinical supervision.* Perhaps you are fortunate enough to be in a clinic or other joint practice setting in which you have regular supervision. Even experienced senior professionals find that such supervision, like other forms of peer review, helps keep them on their toes and up to date.

• *Long-term client follow-up.* Next time you wonder if you're *really* doing any good, look up some former clients and check out how your interventions may be influencing their lives now. Six months, a year, two years later will tell you a great deal about whether you are having the effects you intend. Ask what procedures made the greatest difference, what made the least.... In other words, find out what matters! You may be surprised!

22

ASSESSMENT OF NONSSERTIVE, AGGRESSIVE, AND ASSERTIVE BEHAVIOR

The helping professional who wishes to facilitate social skills must first determine the client's problem and needs. Why has this person sought your help? What's going on?

A thorough assessment is important for at least five reasons:

• To determine if social skills/assertiveness training is the appropriate intervention;

• To determine if you are the appropriate intervener;

• To reach an agreement with the client about her or his exact needs;

• To make an informed decision about the client's readiness for assertiveness or social skills training;

• To adequately individualize the training program.

Assertiveness and social skills training is a versatile tool, but it has limited application. Perhaps the client needs therapy for anxiety, or an intervention for some physical condition. The person may be dealing with spiritual issues, such as guilt or grief or loss. Referral for another specialized or situational condition may be indicated. Thorough assessment helps the facilitator meet specific client needs, and avoid "canning" AT/SST for everyone.

Assertiveness training was first systematized in the 1960's as an individual treatment for anxiety (Wolpe and Lazarus, 1966). The procedure increased in popularity in the early 1970's, parallel to an explosion of interest in group work in the human services. Group assertiveness training had become the "treatment of choice" by the time we released the second edition of *Your Perfect Right* (Alberti and Emmons, 1974). Nevertheless, group training is not appropriate for all clients. In this chapter and in chapters 23-27, we'll take a closer look at how to determine if assertiveness training is indicated, and if so, how to match your interventions to your client's needs.

The client may require services you are not qualified or otherwise able to provide. You cannot help everyone who comes to you, regardless of your talents!

Any type of helping relationship necessarily involves an analysis of client needs. Too often, facilitators either neglect or override the very reasons the person comes for help. Be careful not to foist your values onto clients.

Readiness is also an issue to consider. Perhaps the trainee needs support until a crisis blows over. Some are so shy and withdrawn that even the suggestion of AT/SST triggers physiological reactions or strong emotional resistance. In such cases training would be premature and could be overwhelming to the person.

Some individuals are simply not appropriate candidates for an assertiveness/social skills intervention. The following chapter discusses such contraindications in greater detail. For example, facilitators may wish to hold out of groups those clients who would tend to dominate the nonassertive members.

The fifth consideration, individualizing training, encompasses the points stressed above. An in-depth assessment will help you and your client make better choices about treatment along several dimensions. Social skills are complex. Facilitators who want to maximize the effectiveness of AT/SST interventions must view their clients/trainees from a multivariate perspective.

The following chart, *An Intervention Map for Assessment*, will help you to approach assessment systematically. The trainer may first determine the level of intervention intended (self-help, training, therapy), then measure the trainee's adequacy of (1) information about SST concepts, (2) attitudes toward self-expressive behavior, (3) social skills, and (4,5,6) various obstacles to effective assertiveness in the client's life.

AN INTERVENTION MAP
FOR ASSESSMENT

		Self Help	Training	Therapy
[1] Information	Assessment			
	Intervention			
[2] Attitudes	Assessment			
	Intervention			
[3] Skills	Assessment			
	Intervention			
[4] Environmental Obstacles	Assessment			
	Intervention			
[5] Interpersonal Obstacles	Assessment			
	Intervention			
[6] Intrapersonal Obstacles	Assessment			
	Intervention			

Assessment Methods

There are a variety of ways to gather material concerning the six dimensions noted in the *Intervention Map*. A primary method, of course, is simply listening to the individual describe relationships with others. Carefully explore interactions with (depending upon age and lifestyle) parents, peers, co-workers, classmates, spouse, children, bosses, employees, teachers, salespersons, neighbors, relatives. Who is dominant in these specific relationships? Is the person easily manipulated in dealings with others? Are feelings and ideas openly expressed in most circumstances? Does he or she take advantage of and/or hurt others frequently? What emotional responses are typical?

Wolpe (1969) and Lazarus (1971) suggest questions which are useful in the process of pinpointing responses which are maladaptive for an individual (e.g., "Are you able to contradict a domineering person?"). Responses to such items may be pursued to thoroughly explore the client's nonassertive, aggressive or assertive behavior.

Be sure to cover very personal assertions as well as the more obvious areas. Social behavior is person- and situation-specific, and must be examined in detail, rather than making generalized evaluations about the client's "personality," or artificially generating a global "assertiveness score."

We ask clients to keep ongoing logs or journals, centering around situations, attitudes, behaviors and obstacles (as described in Chapter 3 of *Your Perfect Right*). This is an invaluable source of information regarding assessment of strengths and weaknesses. The log can help the therapist and the client judge ongoing progress.

Standardized Tests Measuring Assertiveness

The emphasis in most AT/SST is on locating current detailed examples of client behavior patterns. For this reason, when we use standardized tests in the diagnostic process, we first look at scores on individual scales, then discuss each item with the client to find out exactly what was meant by the response. The process yields both insights of value in work with the client, and practical experience in the training process. Global scores of "assertiveness" are meaningless, in our opinion. Many scales have been developed which attempt to assess assertiveness directly. One of the most useful is the Gambrill-Richey (1975) *Assertion Inventory*, in which the respondent is asked to report both the "degree of difficulty" in handling a series of situations, and the "response probability" that one will actually attempt to confront that scene. Carol Sacherman (1979) has devised a group assessment approach using the Gambrill-Richey. A group profile is developed which provides a comprehensive view of a single group's needs. The facilitator is then better able to tailor the AT process to the needs of that specific group.

An instrument which offers the most adequate differentiation of different forms of assertiveness is the *Interpersonal Behavior Survey* (Mauger, et al., 1980). In addition, Galassi and Galassi (1980) indicate that combining results on their *College Self-Expression Scale* with those of the *Rathus Assertiveness Schedule* provides comprehensive information about assertiveness measured against behavioral criteria.

Instruments which have been reported in the SST literature include the *Action Situation Inventory* (Friedman, 1971), the *Adolescent Assertion Discrimination Test* (Shoemaker, 1973 as cited in Bodner, 1975), the *Adolescent Self-Expression Scale* (McCarthy & Bellucci, 1974), the *Adult Assertion Scale* (Jakubowski & Wallace, 1975 as cited in Lange & Jakubowski, 1976), the *Adult Self-Expression Scale* (Gay, Hollandsworth & Galassi, 1975), *Anger Self-Report* (Doyle & Biaggio, 1981), the *Assertion Inventory* (Dalali, 1971), the *Assertion Inventory* (Fensterheim, 1971), the *Assertion Inventory* (Gambrill & Richey, 1975), *Assertive Knowledge*

Inventory (Bruch, 1981), the Assertiveness Inventory (Alberti & Emmons, 1974), the AQ Test (Phelps & Austin, 1975), Children's Emotion Projection Instrument (Bernard, 1980), the Cognition Scale of Assertiveness (Golden, 1981), the College Self-Expression Scale (Galassi, DeLo, Galassi & Bastien, 1974), the Conflict Resolution Inventory (McFall & Lillesand, 1971 — designed explicitly to measure refusal behavior), the Constriction Scale (Bates & Zimmerman, 1971), Difficulty in Assertiveness Inventory (Leah, Law & Snyder, 1979), Hypothetical Behavioral Role Playing Assertion Test (Bruch, 1981), Interpersonal Behavior Survey (Mauger, et al., 1980), Interpersonal Problem Solving Assessment Technique (Getter & Nowinski, 1981), the Lawrence Assertive Inventory (Lawrence, 1970), the Modified Rathus Assertiveness Schedule for Children (d'Amico, 1976), the Modified Rathus Assertiveness Schedule for the junior high level (Vaal & McCullagh, 1975), Objective Measure of Assertiveness (Gulanick & Howard, 1979), Personal Relations Inventory (Lorr, More & Mansueto, 1981), Personal Report of Communication Apprehension (Pearson, 1979), the Rathus Assertiveness Schedule (Rathus, 1973), Reduced Behavioral Assertion Test (Bruch, 1981), and the Wolpe-Lazarus Assertiveness Questionnaire (Wolpe and Lazarus, 1966).

We have often been asked about validation studies, scoring procedures, and norms for our Assertiveness Inventory (Chapter 7 of Your Perfect Right). The Inventory is not a validated instrument and has no formalized "scoring" or normative data. It is useful as a clinical tool primarily when the facilitator reviews each item individually with the trainee.

Keep in mind the situation-specific nature of assertiveness, and avoid generalizations based on a "total score" approach!

Behavioral Measures

It can be desirable to employ carefully constructed live behavioral tests to determine the degree of a client's difficulty with assertiveness. Assessment may be based on post-situation self report, expert judgements of performance, and physiological measures of anxiety. Audio and video tape recording devices are useful in sampling client behaviors in these situations. Examples applying such approaches are given in McFall and Marston (1970), Friedman (1971), and Eisler, Miller, and Hersen (1973). Another valuable contribution to behavioral measures is the "unobtrusive" approach of Cummins (1978).

At least two studies (Gorecki, et al., 1981; Howard, et al., 1980) question the validity of the "behavioral" measures taken in laboratory or therapy settings, suggesting great caution when attempting to assess probable *in vivo* behavior by observing responses in unrealistic environments, such as role play tests.

Cognitive Measures

To measure the influence of attitudes and obstacles for a given client, cognitive assessment instruments can give insight into the client's thoughts reactive to situations calling for self-expression. Stefanek and Eisler (1983) have identified several cognitive components as key areas to assess in assertiveness training: self-statements, knowledge of appropriate assertive behavior, anticipation of consequences, irrational beliefs, and social anxiety.

Self-statements (self-talk, internal dialogue, automatic thoughts) either inhibit or facilitate one's assertive responses: e.g. "I'll feel embarrassed if I say no" vs. "I have the right to say no." An instrument developed specifically for assessing self-statements is the *Assertive Self-Statement Test* (ASST), Schwartz and Gottman (1976). The ASST contains sixteen positive thoughts believed to facilitate refusal responses and sixteen negative thoughts believed to inhibit refusal responses. The SPCI contains lists of positive and negative consequences that could result from complying with or refusing an unreasonable request. A factor analysis of these two instruments was recently conducted by Bruch, Haase and Purcell (1984).

Knowledge of appropriate behavior (the ability to distinguish between assertive, non-assertive, and aggressive actions) may be assessed by the *Assertive Knowledge Inventory* (Schwartz and Gottman, 1976). This device requires individuals to write out an appropriate refusal response to unreasonable requests.

Anticipation of consequences refers to the thoughts one has about what might happen as a direct result of behaving assertively. Fiedler and Beach (1978) devised the *Subjective Probability of Consequences Inventory* (SPCI) to measure these types of cognitions. Eisler, Frederiksen and Peterson (1978) created several instruments for the same purpose, including the *Generalized Expectations of Others Questionnaire* (GEOQ).

Irrational beliefs — the idea that distorted beliefs hinder assertive responses (and other emotionally healthy actions) — derives largely from the work of Albert Ellis (Ellis and Harper, 1979) and Aaron Beck (1976, et al. 1979). A key measuring instrument is the *Irrational Beliefs Test* (IBT), Jones (1968). The IBT is a 100-item factor analyzed self-report inventory. It measures the rationality-irrationality of ten beliefs identified by Ellis. In a study by Cash (1984), the total score on the IBT correlated significantly with reported social assertiveness.

Social anxiety is the fear some individuals have of possible rejection or negative evaluation by others in social situations. Such anxiety can be a powerful inhibitor of appropriate assertive behavior, and its assessment is a key to successful interventions. Watson and Friend (1969) developed two early scales which can be useful: the *Social Avoidance and Distress Scale (SAD)*, and the *Fear of Negative Evaluation Scale*. The *Gambrill-Richey Assertion Inventory* (1975) also has subjects rate their degree of anxiety in situations calling for assertiveness. There are a number of standardized personality tests that can be helpful in measurement of obstacles to self-expression, including the *Edwards Personal Preference Schedule*, the *Eysenk Personality Inventory*, and the *Myers-Briggs Type Indicator*. Some of the anxiety and fear measures of value are the *Taylor Manifest Anxiety Scale*, the *Willoughby Schedule* (Wolpe, 1958; Hestand, 1971), and the *Fear Survey Schedule* (Wolpe and Lang, 1969).

Reviews of AT Assessment Devices

Vagg (1979) edited a special issue of the now-defunct *ASSERT* newsletter on the topic of assessment, including a useful critique of methods and criteria for evaluating an instrument. He suggests first determining what type of information about client social functioning you are seeking, then deciding which particular instrument will satisfy those needs. In determining the value of an instrument, find out if there is a test manual (or reasonable substitute) available. Third, how much time will it take to administer and to interpret the results? Tests should be brief and flexible enough to be completed quickly. Other considerations are the populations used for standardization, the reading level of the test, and the presence of safeguards for defensiveness and/or honesty.

Bodner (1975) provided a detailed review of early assessment in AT, including paper-and-pencil, observational, and behavioral measures. Galassi and Galassi (1977) also prepared an extensive discussion of AT assessment, with guidelines for developing an individualized scale.

St. Lawrence (1987) has classified a wide variety of assertiveness instruments within the categories: tests assessing knowledge of assertive behavior; behavioral interviews; self-report inventories and questionnaires; behavioral components of assertion (verbal and non-verbal); behavioral role-play assessment; behavioral records by the trainee; contrived situations; physiological assessment. In her summary statement, St. Lawrence points out that "the assessment of assertion is an evolving technology"— a conclusion not unlike that of Galassi and Galassi (1977) a decade earlier: "...progress in developing and refining the technique has outstripped progress in developing measures of assertive behavior and in evaluating the effects..."

The *Principles for Ethical Practice of Assertive Behavior Training* (Appendix C of *Your Perfect Right*) describes seven dimensions which should be evaluated in determining the appropriateness and level of an AT/SST intervention: *client, problem/goals, facilitator, setting, time/duration, method, outcome.* Trainers are urged to become familiar with these guidelines.

Holistic Assessment

Any client may need a more thorough assessment and treatment program than a social skills approach alone can provide. AT/SST is a powerful way to help, but the facilitator should be prepared to assess client needs along holistic lines in order to offer more responsible and thorough treatment and/or referral.

The word "holistic" refers to the entire, complete, whole. It points to assessing and treating one as thoroughly as possible: psychologically, physically, spiritually, environmentally. This is a virtually impossible task for the mental health worker acting alone. It will usually require a stretch beyond one's training, or beyond the scope of an institutional program. Yet, if we are to respond fully to the needs of our clients, it is necessary to look beyond a presenting complaint of "social inadequacy."

Assessment interviews can include questions about physical history and present functioning, spiritual history and present functioning, environments and relationships at home and at work. Certain clients may have physical disorders which contribute to their nonassertive or aggressive behavior. Michael Emmons has helped uncover anemia, mononucleosis, hypoglycemia and pre-menstrual syndrome in a number of cases. It can be very difficult to be socially effective when your physical health is severely lacking!

There is currently a great deal of interest in the biological roots of disorders that have been traditionally viewed as psychological, including anxiety or panic attacks, depression, schizophrenia, obsessive compulsive disorders. The etiology in many such cases is directly traceable to physical factors. The January, 1986, issue of the American Psychological Association newspaper, *Monitor*, discussed the explosive impact of the neurosciences on psychology, including important implications for cognitive psychology, psychopharmacology, clinical practice, and behavioral medicine. Yale neuroscientist Patricia Goldman-Rakic was quoted: "Nature is unified and you have to understand it in its entirety."

Rippere (1983), in a paper on "Nutritional Approaches to Behavior Modification," reports support for including diet information as a standard part of the intake interview. Her review covers the nutritional treatment of such conditions as agoraphobia, learning disorders, mental retardation, alcoholism, anxiety states, and hyperactivity.

Many physical difficulties manifest as psychological symptoms. Become knowledgeable about the whole person and your social skills/assertiveness training will be more successful.

The spiritual side of the client's condition also has direct implications for mental health workers. Key issues such as guilt (real and neurotic), anger and aggression, meekness and humbleness, "turning the other cheek," and love may be vital elements of the cognitive predisposition of a client. Spiritual belief systems may contribute to positive, uplifting, confirming attitudes as well.

While environmental influences on behavior are extremely difficult to isolate, more and more information is becoming available, and a thorough assessment can include appropriate questions about working and living conditions, economic circumstances, discrimination, environmental health factors, social and peer pressures, and other considerations "outside" the individual.

All of us want simplistic answers to "what's wrong" in our lives. But we humans are not simple beings. Different interventions work with different people. Genuinely holistic methods — including traditional and alternative medicine, exercise, nutrition, psychological treatment, spiritual development, life/career changes, environmental interventions — allow for those differences, and assess and treat the complex person in a comprehensive, holistic manner.

Holistic assessment will expand your treatment approach, but may lead you beyond your own expertise. Be willing to stretch your vision of the client toward broader horizons, but work within your own strengths and limitations. Referral will often be the most appropriate alternative — to other mental health professionals, medical or alternative health care professionals, and religious or spiritual advisers. Exercise appropriate ethical caution, and avoid the hazards of the "supertherapist trap" — trying to be all things for all clients. It is very rewarding to successfully help others, but it is necessary to temper holistic concern with common sense and ethical restraint. Approach and assess your clients holistically, but avoid the temptation to try to cure everybody of everything that ails them.

23

LIMITATIONS AND CONTRAINDICATIONS

You've carefully assessed your client's needs and determined that social skills training is the correct intervention, right? Great, but before you reach for your bag of AT/SST tricks, there is one more hurdle you must clear. What steps have you taken to consider the limitations and possible contraindications for training with this person? How have you decided whether to refer to individual or group training? What level of intervention are you recommending: Self-help? Training? Therapy?

The careful practice of assertiveness and social skills training requires consideration to these matters as you respond to the needs of each client. Several specific steps will help insure that your training is conducted with appropriate consideration for the limitations and contraindications of the procedure. (This is brief and to-the-point, so don't skip over the next few pages!)

Client Considerations

• Carefully consider whether a given client should be in individual or group work (see Chapter 26).

• Highly anxious types (see Chapters 10 and 22) should be treated for anxiety first.

• The evidence is mixed about whether schizophrenics are good candidates. Familiarize yourself with the literature in this area if you will be working with that population, or if it is likely that you will come across schizophrenia in a walk-in setting.

• Individuals with extremely limited verbal skills will need specially-adapted social skills training, individually or in homogeneous groups, and only when it is indicated by their needs and readiness. Proceed carefully.

• Persons who are unable to perceive the responses of others (i.e. those who are insensitive, dull, lacking in social discrimination skills or awareness,...) should be referred for work on interpersonal sensitivity before AT/SST.

• Unmotivated clients are unlikely to make progress in any training or therapy environment, and may discourage other participants in an AT/SST group.

• Actively resistant clients are likely to take a great deal of energy and to make little progress. If your setting can afford it, you may make important strides with AT/SST, but it will be costly in time and energy. As with the unmotivated, take care not to permit such individuals to discourage others who want to work.

• Screen out extremely aggressive individuals who will disrupt groups. (It can be very rewarding to work with such persons individually, however, and to prepare them for group membership.)

• While there is no clear evidence of contraindication, common sense says decline sociopaths, unless you are treating them in an institutional setting.

Trainer Considerations

Your limitations as a trainer set parameters, too. AT/SST can be conducted as education, as skill building, or as therapy. The depth of your interventions should be limited to those procedures which you are qualified to administer.

• The demands and expectations of a trainer employed by a company to coach employees for improved job performance are very different from those of one who works independently as a therapist offering long-term behavioral change. Stay within the limits of your setting.

• Please note the qualifications for trainers and therapists listed in Appendix C.

Procedural Considerations

In the sweep of assertiveness training's popularity in the 1970s, many folks got the idea that here was an appropriate intervention for all kinds of people with all kinds of needs. It helped with anxiety, social inadequacy, shyness, depression, job advancement, overcoming oppression, political change, child development, marital relationships, parenting, organizational leadership.... The search for quick answers seemed to have ended for some.

Fortunately, it was not long before the limitations of the technique became evident. Here are a few:

• The definition of assertiveness remains a stumbling block.

• The structure of social skills training, as a systematic behavioral procedure, may not satisfy the desire of many persons for "insight" and understanding of their difficulties.

• Research evidence suggests that transfer of learning from the training environment to the trainee's life circumstances may be very limited. In any event, it is necessary for the trainer to take steps to maximize transfer of training. Developing "good group members" is not your goal.

• Procedures in AT/SST are often unclear, untested, little understood by trainers themselves. Many trainers use questionable notions of individual "rights" and teach forms of selfish behavior which disregard the effects upon others in the trainee's environment. It is very common for trainers to use "canned" procedures uniformly for all persons, rather than individualizing the training according to the needs of the participants. (We are reminded once again of the "go into a restaurant and ask for a glass of water" form of homework assignment. Not cool, folks.)

• Social skills training is a complex process which demands attention to the client's attitudes and beliefs, anxiety, behavioral skills, and obstacles which inhibit self-expression. Many clients, and more than a few trainers as well, would prefer to engage in a few "role-plays" of difficult situations, and pronounce themselves "assertive" or "socially competent." If that's your approach, we hope you'll get serious about the power of AT/SST procedures — or maybe give up AT altogether and find another procedure to misuse.

Social skills and assertiveness training, however comprehensively applied, remains one procedure in the therapist's repertoire of tools for working with clients. No more a "cure all" than any other approach, its limitations must be carefully observed. Apply it carefully, within a context defined by the client's needs and life circumstances, your own limitations, and the parameters of the training setting.

24

TECHNIQUES AND PROCEDURES FOR ASSERTIVENESS TRAINING

Let's begin to get specific about appropriate and effective procedures for assertiveness training. This chapter and the next two offer guidelines for applying the material presented in *Your Perfect Right* to the needs of your clients. *It is assumed that you are thoroughly familiar with the material in that volume, and are qualified as described in Chapter 21.*

Client Preparation

In *Your Perfect Right*, we discussed some basic elements of assertive motivation and attitude development. The process of preparation for assertive living is essentially the same for trainer or client. Familiarity with the differences among nonassertive, aggressive, and assertive behaviors is a foundation which is prerequisite for the steps which follow.

To prepare your clients/trainees, therefore, we suggest you assign *Your Perfect Right* or another appropriate book for preparatory reading on the subject. Then the concepts should be discussed at some length. Often such a discussion is more effective in a group session, whether or not the training itself will be conducted in a group.

A few clients will get started simply from *exposure* to the AT concepts and recognition that there are alternatives to nonassertion or aggression. Nevertheless, we suggest a "trial run" with you, so you may assess the adequacy of the trainee's style before the "real world" is tackled. Even though some individuals may not need a full training program, it is wise for the facilitator to check out skills and anxiety. One useful tool in the process of confirming the level of client performance is the "method of contrasted role plays" (MacNeilage and Adams, 1977).

Those clients who will be started on a full AT program, whether individual or group, should be informed fully of the procedures which will be employed, and outcomes to be expected (again, refer to the *Principles* in Appendix C).

Overcoming Internal Obstacles

In every client's life there are obstacles to self- expression. Some obstacles are within the person, some are in the person's life situation, but everyone has to deal with them. Internal obstacles fall into two major categories: *anxiety* and *cognitions* (attitudes and beliefs). Let's take a look at some typical internal obstacles faced by AT clients, and ways to work with them in assertiveness training.

Anxiety. This is, of course, the most common (and most easily treated) of the internal obstacles to assertiveness. It must be regarded seriously, particularly by those trainers not trained in dealing with serious psychological problems. We suggest the following procedures:

• Do some type of systematic assessment of anxiety levels for all your clients/trainees. Get the help of a trained psychologist if you are not qualified.

- Accept into training only those whose anxiety is within an acceptable range.
- Refer for treatment any whose anxiety level is particularly high. (We recommend a behavioral or cognitive-behavioral psychologist for this procedure.)
- If your qualifications allow, treat the client directly for anxiety, using appropriate methods of measurement, identification and classification of the fears, and desensitization or cognitive procedures.
- Some clients will respond to guided imagery or other covert treatments for anxiety.
- Do not make treatment of anxiety a part of assertiveness training *per se.*
- Do not attempt systematic desensitization without necessary qualifications and specific training in that procedure.
- Stress inoculation techniques are appropriate coping tools which can be taught within the context of AT, including such appropriate self-statements as:

"I'm going to encounter a stress situation."

"I can handle it."

"The anxiety will pass."

"A wise person would do this..."

- If more intensive therapy is indicated, for anxiety or other psychological difficulties, make an appropriate referral as soon as practical.

Attitudes and Beliefs. Actions and feelings are profoundly influenced by attitudes, beliefs, and thoughts. Assertiveness trainers must:

- recognize and acknowledge the effects of cognitive elements on the way one responds to the world, and
- be prepared to aid clients in changing counter-productive thinking.

Belief systems take many forms, of course. Social,

educational, cultural, and religious organizations are very influential, as is the family. Society and its institutions foster ideas and attitudes which serve their purposes, such as "our country is better than other countries."

Four social myths responsible for much nonassertive behavior have been described by *Sherwin Cotler* and *Julio Guerra* (1976). The myths of *anxiety, obligation, modesty,* and the *good friend* help to explain typical belief systems which inhibit self-assertion. Trainee understanding of the false premises inherent in these myths can do much to free them to attempt assertions.

A number of researchers and clinicians have developed systematic procedures for helping clients to deal with faulty beliefs, irrational ideas, and other cognitions not in their own best interests. Among the leaders in this field are Aaron Beck (1979), Albert Ellis (1980), Gary Emery (1984), Arnold Lazarus (1981), and Donald Meichenbaum (1977).

Beck (1979) has identified a particularly comprehensive list of cognitive therapy procedures:

Activity scheduling
Ascertaining meanings
Cognitive rehearsal
Diversion procedures
Eliciting and testing automatic thoughts
Focusing and concentration practice
Graded task assignments
Guided imagery
Homework assignments
Mastery and pleasure ratings
Reattribution.

Beck, however, views cognitive therapy more as a matter of helping clients to "become their own therapists" than as a collection of techniques. He emphasizes the roles of biological, behavioral, mood, *and* cognitive factors in the development of emotional responses.

Cognitive interventions focus attention on thoughts and assumptions about life situations, and attempt to lead the client toward constructive thinking, emotions, and behavior. Typical steps in a cognitive approach include:
• Determining the "automatic thoughts" which occur in response to a stimulus situation;
• Examining the thoughts, and underlying assumptions, to determine their appropriateness;
• Applying cognitive procedures (eg. list above) to modifying the assumptions, so they become positive, realistic, rational, and functional;
• Teaching clients how to evaluate and modify thoughts and assumptions on their own, after therapy.

In Chapter 9 of *Your Perfect Right*, we discussed three specific cognitive procedures for dealing with self-defeating thoughts: stress inoculation, thought-stopping, and positive self-statements. Trainers are urged to review that material.

Overcoming External Obstacles

Obstacles outside the person can be even more resistant to change than those within. Therapists are familiar with many therapeutic procedures which can be employed to help clients change themselves. How can we help them bring about change in their environments?

Life circumstances of clients will inevitably determine how much freedom they really have to make changes. Socio-economic conditions, institutional discrimination (gender, age, race, handicap), education, and geographic environment are among the influences in everyone's life which are difficult or impossible to change. What the facilitator can hope to do is to become sensitive to these and other factors which face clients in any attempt to change, and to help them to develop tools for working with those givens.

Assertiveness itself, of course, is such a tool. Good information — and how to find it — is another. Contacts with local resources which can help with civil rights laws, tenants rights, public assistance programs, educational opportunities, job resources, anti-discrimination regulations and more ought to be part of the counselor's repertoire. Public libraries are storehouses of an amazing variety of information which can help you and your clients to deal with the hassles and hurdles of the bureaucracy. A useful resource is *Surviving America*, a handbook of what's available and how to get it, developed by the Center for Third World Organizing of Oakland, California (1984).

If you'll prepare yourself to be of help in these areas, your clients will have a much greater chance of bringing about the changes in their lives which assertiveness can make possible.

Significant others in the client's life pose another external obstacle which usually is not within direct reach of the human services professional. Spouse, parents, other family members, boss, roommate(s), co-workers, and others can make it very difficult for the client to apply skills learned in your training sessions.

An element of these relationships which must be carefully considered is that of trust. In some cases (a minority, we believe) those closest to the client have a vested interest in making increased assertiveness difficult. Usually the client is aware of the potential sabotage, and is reluctant to trust that person with the knowledge of therapy or other efforts to change.

Trainers must exercise some caution in pushing clients to confront such difficult associates until a considerable level of assertive skill has been developed. Help Jane get *ready* to take on her husband before you urge her on. Give Fred a gentle shove toward "shaping up" his domineering mother, but let *him* decide how fast to move in this very sensitive area.

Skill Training With Components of Behavior

The heart of assertiveness training from its inception has been the development of effective behavioral skills. For a considerable period in the early 1970s, "assertiveness" was — unfortunately, in our opinion — virtually synonymous with the capacity to look someone in the eye and tell him or her off. While the popular conception of assertiveness has broadened considerably, skills training is still at the core of the process.

Effective skills training with the components of behavior includes several specific procedures: modeling, imagery rehearsal, anxiety management, cognitive procedures, behavior rehearsal, feedback, coaching, practice, and homework. The step-by-step process described in detail in Chapter 12 demonstrates how these procedures are applied. Here we'll examine them from the trainer's perspective. In the next chapter, we'll show how they fit into your work with individuals, and in Chapter 25 you'll see them in action in a group. The components, you will recall from Chapter 6, are eye contact, body posture, distance/contact, facial expression, gestures, voice tone, voice inflection, voice volume, fluency, timing, listening, thoughts, and content.

Let's take a look at the skills training procedures one-by-one:

Modeling: Albert Bandura (1969) and others have demonstrated conclusively that humans constantly imitate the behavior they observe in others. As young children, we all learned language, posture, expression, and style by watching our parents, teachers, and older peers. This important characteristic of human learning can be a valuable tool in social skills training. Use it! Teach your trainees to be good observers of others. Give them criteria for judging effective behavior and for choosing good models.

Imagery Rehearsal: There is a considerable body of evidence that we can teach ourselves new skills about as well

by *imagining* progress as by *practice* in the "real world."
Cautela's (1974) research in particular, and more recent work
by Fensterheim (1980), Kazdin (1982), and Suinn (1985),
points to the value of encouraging trainees to stop for a
moment, close their eyes, and imagine themselves behaving
appropriately and enjoying success in handling a situation.

Anxiety Management: Assertiveness training was
originally developed as a procedure for counterconditioning
anxiety. Indeed, AT does reduce anxiety levels for many
trainees. Those with high levels of anxiety, however, will need
additional work with specific anxiety reduction methods, such
as systematic desensitization, stress inoculation, thought
stopping and other cognitive behavioral stress reduction
methods. We suggest a systematic assessment of anxiety to
help screen those trainees who need anxiety reduction treatment before they continue in assertiveness training. Please
refer to Chapter 10 of *Your Perfect Right.*

Cognitive Restructuring: A high level of behavioral skill
alone will not lead to effective action if the person's thoughts,
beliefs, and attitudes are saying, "No way!" With many
individuals it is necessary to overcome such self-imposed
barriers as irrational beliefs ("The other person will hate
me!"), negative self-statements ("I just know I'm going to
make a fool of myself!"), and self-limiting attitudes ("I have
no right to talk back to this person.").

Read Chapter 9, and the material on "Attitudes and
Beliefs" earlier in this chapter. Study the work of Ellis (1980),
Beck (1986), Meichenbaum (1977), and others. We do not
believe that "your perfect rights" include all of the self-serving
ideas which have been advocated in the name of "assertiveness," or that a personal "bill of rights" is necessary. We do,
however, strongly encourage trainers to work with the cognitive dimension, and to teach clients methods for developing
positive outlooks on behavior and relationships.

Behavior Rehearsal: This step, of course, has been the heart of the social skills training process since the earliest days of AT. Here we get the trainees off their chairs, trying out their skills in staged scenes, and showing themselves and the trainer what they can do. For many, extra support and encouragement is needed at this point to overcome real or feigned embarrassment at being observed. And observation is critical. The trainer (and other trainees in a group setting) must watch carefully the specific components of the trainee's behavior and be prepared to give helpful feedback.

Feedback: Now a sample of the trainee's behavior is available, and she wants to know what went well and where improvement is needed. Effective observation by the trainer and other students, and/or audio or video tape must be communicated to each trainee. Feedback is most valuable when it is most specific. Pay attention to each of the components of the trainee's behavior in turn. It can help, in a group, to assign one component to each group member for observation, especially in the early meetings. This teaches everyone the importance of specific component feedback. (Review Chapter 6.)

Coaching: Here we are applying the previous two procedures, behavior rehearsal and feedback, with active trainer intervention to help trainees shape their behavior more closely to the goals they have set for themselves. Few training environments allow enough time to carry out this step adequately, but it can be approximated in group training by structuring triads in which trainees may coach each other. (More on this in Chapter 25.)

Practice: Behavior skills which are developed through the procedures described above will only become a permanent part of the trainee's repertoire through repeated *practice*. Psychologist/educator Uvaldo Palomares tells a story of his own early experiences in the cotton fields of Southern California. Small in stature, Palomares often found himself denied access to the fullest rows of cotton by larger, more aggressive youths. He looked for the "best way to fight," so he could hold his own with the bullies, and thus earn more. He decided Karate was the answer, memorized the best book he could find on the subject, and tried it out on one of his nemeses. Within thirty seconds, he says with a sheepish grin, he was rolling in the dirt as always, overpowered by his larger enemy. As he points out, "In a crisis, we go back to the ways which are most natural to us." What happened to his Karate? He had neglected to *practice* the techniques, to make the new skills a part of himself. Be sure your social skills trainees don't make the same mistake.

Homework: One effective means to encourage your trainees to practice their new skills is to give specific homework assignments to be carried out between sessions. (Shelton and Ackerman, 1974, offer a thorough discussion of this topic.) Such assignments should be appropriate to the clients' level of skills, and coordinated with the training to maximize the likelihood of success. Don't send your clients out to take on more than they can handle! Even minor failures during training can represent a considerable setback. Encourage them to focus on specific components — one at a time at first. Increase the difficulty of homework gradually, just as you do with in-session training: from staged practice with friends, to *in vivo* situations with strangers, to spontaneous interaction with intimates. Encourage log-keeping, and make micro-cassette recorders available if possible, so you can offer feedback later.

Formats for Assertiveness Training

AT has had quite a colorful history, as therapeutic techniques go. It has been applied in virtually every setting imaginable: individual therapy, group therapy, workshops, classrooms, on the job,... It has often been offered as a stand-alone procedure (particularly in the early days), and often integrated into another context, such as an employee development program or a broad therapeutic intervention.

In determining the most appropriate formats for training, there are dimensions which go beyond the trainer's convenience. Here is a list for your consideration:

• Your basic goal ought to be to individualize the training as much as possible, moving clients from where they are to where they want or need to be. That requires careful assessment, and design of interventions which will accomplish the goals effectively and efficiently.

• Benefits of individual AT are:

...personal attention

...opportunity for more intensive work

...opportunity for combining AT with other interventions

...less threatening environment for some clients

• Problems with individual work:

...more threatening for some clients, due to the intensity and "therapy" setting

...there is only a single source for feedback and coaching

...the client may learn to deal with only one person.

• Benefits of group training:

...greater variety of persons for interaction

...more realistic environment

...more sources of feedback and coaching

...more social models

...larger and more powerful support system.

• Problems of group training:

...less individual attention from trainer

...more threatening for some clients (exposure, "public performance")

...needs of members may vary considerably

...groups may seem to be the real world, but are not.

• Benefits of workshop training:

...easily accessible

...usually least expensive

...less threatening and less intensive.
• Problems of workshop training:
...little individual attention from facilitator
...usually emphasizes didactic over experiential
...suitable only as an introductory exposure.

Intact vs. Ad Hoc Groups

Most assertiveness training takes place within a context established by the trainer: a clinical office, a group therapy program, a weekend workshop — all *ad hoc* settings established for the training itself. Our discussions of procedure thus far have largely assumed that context.

Occasionally an opportunity will come up to work with trainees in their *own* environment — an *intact* group. Once again, it can be important to give some thought to how external factors — the setting in this case — influence the process. Intact groups may be as small as a committed couple, or as large as the staff of a company.

With intimate intact groups, the trainer must recognize the long term consequences of any intervention. As with marriage and family counseling, you are dealing with the most significant relationships in the lives of your trainees. Great sensitivity to their needs is critical. Never forget that they — and not you — will live with the consequences of what happens for the rest of their lives.

If you push intimates or family members to greater assertiveness with one another, you probably will enhance their communication and improve the functioning of their relationships. You may also lead them to divorce or long term estrangement. Be prepared to work with the relationship in depth before you begin, and use AT only as one tool in a carefully considered overall plan of intervention.

A few guidelines:
...gain everyone's informed consent to participation
...focus on current interactions; stay away from history

...try to bring non-verbal behavior to the verbal level

...identify current life cycle issues in the family

...identify underlying belief systems (i.e. cultural) which may inhibit assertiveness

...help family members figure out their individual goals

...help family members identify the emotions that are obstacles to assertiveness

...help family members identify the way they encourage/inhibit each other's self-expression

...keep an eye on the family *system*, and how this intervention will likely affect its functioning

...build a reinforcement network in the family, to help them help each other.

When you work within a larger intact framework, such as a work group, a residential community (eg. university residence hall), or another social system, there are other considerations:

...keep in mind that, while the commitment is not so long-term as that of a family, these people will go on working or living together after you leave

...establish appropriate outcome goals for the training. (Whose idea was this anyway? The boss? The dean? The members themselves?)

...gain informed — and voluntary! — consent

...establish clear ground rules

...make every effort to assess probable changes in the organizational system as an outcome of the intervention. (Is the system strong enough to handle the changes?)

Failures in Assertiveness Training

Unfortunately, assertiveness training is not always successful. It can be tough to admit, but failure can be quite instructive if one takes it seriously as a learning opportunity. Several authors have recently addressed this sensitive issue.

Emmons and Alberti (1983) discuss failures due to inadequacies in the AT model, inappropriate referral, inadequate assessment, and client characteristics.

Goldstein-Fodor and Epstein (1983) deal with a wide variety of failures specifically relating to women clients. Their long list includes failure of self-report measures to delineate the specific nature of "women's assertiveness deficit," failure to assess behavior relevant to women's real-life issues, failure to define criteria for successful assertiveness, failure to determine "appropriate assertive" responses, failure of training methods, failure to prepare women for new roles, failure of cognitive restructuring to counter real discrimination, failure to study nonassertive "effective" female behaviors, failures in generalization, failure to follow-up clients, failure to assess the impact of assertiveness training on "significant others," and various AT-related therapist and group variables.

Ruben and Ruben (1989) point to three primary difficulties of AT programs, based on consumer complaints and on an analysis of current research in the field: (1) the negative image of AT; (2) curriculum failures due to ambiguous definitions, inconsistent teaching models, inferior background of trainers; and (3) generalizability of results.

And you thought AT was simple!

One of the difficulties with facilitation of assertiveness is that it is *deceptively* simple. One can *do* AT relatively easily. To do it responsibly, thoroughly, and ethically takes more thought, preparation, sensitivity to client needs, and planning.

Please avoid shortcut approaches.

25

INDIVIDUAL TRAINING PROCEDURES

(Before you begin this chapter, take a few minutes to return to Chapter 12 of *Your Perfect Right*, and re-read the self-directed process.)

Here is a step-by-step description of a "typical" AT intervention with an individual client:

Step 1: Be certain you are adequately prepared as a facilitator.

Review Chapter 21 and the statement of *Principles for Ethical Practice of Assertive Behavior Training*. Please do not attempt to conduct assertiveness training unless you have the necessary qualifications.

Step 2: Do a thorough preliminary assessment of the needs of the client.

Review chapters 6, 8 and 22. Select an appropriate assessment procedure for the client, and implement it. Avoid global measures of "assertiveness." Pay careful attention to anxiety assessment to judge an appropriate level of situation with which to begin. It is a good idea to have the client rank-order specific troublesome situations calling for self-expression. Begin with those that will provoke only manageable anxiety.

Step 3: Identify a situation that needs attention.
The following example will illustrate the next several steps:

> *Client*: A man at work has asked me out several times and he just won't take my hints. I don't want to hurt his feelings by telling him the truth. What should I do? I'm certain he will ask me again.

Step 4: Set up the scene.
Work with the client to structure closely the practice situation, in order to understand the situation fully, to be able to present the scene accurately for covert and behavioral rehearsal, and to simulate the feelings she has in the real situation.

> *Facilitator*: You've decided you don't like him?
>
> *Client*: No, he's a nice person, but we just don't have the same interests. Besides, I'm not attracted to him physically. I can't tell him that, though; it would crush him.
>
> *Facilitator*: What makes you think he couldn't handle it? Tell me some more about him and what he has said to you....

Step 5: Deal with cognitive issues.
Discuss the client's beliefs about how things *ought* to be, her perceptions of what others are thinking, any irrational beliefs about her effect on others, etc. In the example, the facilitator should focus particularly on her statements: "I don't want to hurt his feelings" and "It would crush him."

Work to help restructure thoughts, attitudes, beliefs. (Refer to Chapter 9, *Your Perfect Right.*)

Client: Harold — that's his name — seems to be a pretty wimpy person.

Facilitator: And you think you have a responsibility to be careful not to hurt him?

Client: I don't want to be mean!

Facilitator: So you think it is wrong to be honest with people, to be sure you don't *ever* take the risk of hurting anyone?

Client: I see what you mean. I guess I can't always go around walking on eggs so I won't hurt anybody.

Step 6: Structure the scene for covert rehearsal.

Facilitator: I'd like for you to go over the situation in your imagination now. Close your eyes and imagine yourself talking to him again. Let yourself respond in whatever way you feel.

Client: (Silent, imagines scene.)

Step 7: Help the client develop positive self-statements.

Facilitator: Tell me what you were saying to yourself in your imagination.

Client: At first I thought, "I *can't* do this!" Then I saw the scene, and thought, "Oh, poor Harold. He really needs me. I *mustn't* tell him no; it would kill him!"

Facilitator: So, first you thought, "I can't," then you thought, "I mustn't."

Client: Yes, that's right.

Facilitator: Try to replace those thoughts with positive ones. Can you think of some good ones?

At this point you may need to do further cognitive restructuring and help the client work through some faulty attitudes and beliefs. Be careful to balance the available time between

cognitive interventions and behavioral practice. Assign
cognitive homework as needed.

Step 8: Model an assertive response for the situation.
Present audio and video models if available. You may wish
to videotape your modeling here also, so the client can view
it again as needed.

Facilitator: Let me show you *one* way to approach
him. Pretend I am you and you are Harold.

Client: Okay, I'll try....(As Harold) Hi, ...(*small
talk*)...Say, there is a great movie playing downtown, and
I would love to have you go with me on Friday. I'll be so
disappointed if you can't go.

Facilitator (as client): I really am busy on Friday, but
I've been wanting to talk to you about us, Harold. I feel
I have been misleading you, and I want to straighten
things out. I really don't want to hurt you, but I don't see
any future in our relationship.

Client: Why? What have I done wrong?

Facilitator: That's just it; you've done nothing wrong.
I feel that our interests aren't the same, and I'm not
really attracted to you.

Client: Oh, ...

Facilitator: I hope you aren't too disappointed, but I
had to be honest with you, so I wouldn't hurt you more
later.

Client: Well, I appreciate *that* anyway. So, I guess I
shouldn't ask you anymore?

Facilitator: That would be best....

*Step 9: Answer the client's questions about how you hand-
led the situation.*
Point out the differences between assertive, nonassertive
and aggressive responses. Stress pertinent non-verbal factors. Discuss further philosophical concerns.

Client: You sounded so "perfect!" Sometimes I really don't know what I *want* in a situation. What if I'm not sure?

Facilitator: Not sure whether you want to go out with him?

Client: No, I'm not sure how I feel about him, except I know I don't want to date him.

Facilitator: Could you say that... what you just told me?

Client: You mean tell him I'm not sure how I feel, but I don't want to go out?

Facilitator: Yes.

Client: I guess that's being pretty up-front! But what if he's real persistent?

Facilitator: That is a possibility. I would stay assertive. Stay with your basic message.

Client: Wouldn't it be better to tell white lies like, "I have to wash my hair," so he'll get the hint?

Facilitator: You've tried hints already and they haven't worked. Even if they eventually did work, you actually are hurting him and yourself more in the long run by not being honest with your feelings. Believe me, ninety-nine guys out of a hundred would rather you told them the truth, even though it hurts at the time!

Step 10: Repeat Step 6.
Repeat covert rehearsal, this time encouraging the client to visualize a successful outcome based on effective model.

Step 11: Rehearse the scene once again.
This time the client role-plays herself. Audio or video tape if possible. Interrupt immediately if gross errors are evident. Do a "mini-model," focusing on the problem area and have the person practice it several times. Lengthen the scene as confidence is gained.

Facilitator: Hold it. Let's stop for a moment. Did you hear yourself say, "Maybe sometime..."? That's not fair to him unless you really think the situation might change. Do you?

Client: No, I was just trying to let him down easy.

Facilitator: Stay honest! "Letting him down easy" is holding out false hope. Okay? Let's try it again.

Step 12: Go over the performance.

Provide feedback and coaching where needed. Focus on nonverbal elements — eye contact, voice qualities, posture — as well as the content of the message. Offer much positive feedback. Emphasize self-reinforcement:

Facilitator: You did an excellent job! I liked the way you stuck to your point when he tried to persuade you. Your eye contact was good. Your voice was a little soft and somewhat shaky, but you hung in there. Let's do it again. Try to use a stronger voice this time. And remind yourself how well you're doing as it goes along.

Step 13: Repeat Steps 7 through 12 as often as needed.

Alternate between modeling and role-playing, and provide coaching to shape the behavior to the *client's* satisfaction, as much as time allows.

Step 14: The client is now ready to test the new response pattern in the actual situation.

Up to this point the preparation has taken place in the relatively secure training environment. Nevertheless, careful training and repeated practice have developed the person's ability to respond more adequately to the situation. Offer necessary reassurance and encourage her to proceed *in vivo*. If she is unwilling to do so, further rehearsals, or perhaps treatment for anxiety, may be needed. Also, ask to hear the positive self-statements she is thinking.

Facilitator: How do you feel about using your new approach with him when he calls again?
Client: I think I'm ready, and I know he's going to call.
Facilitator: Well, I feel good about how you've handled it here, so I also think you're ready. Tell me what you're saying to yourself now, as you act the scene....

Step 15: Encourage the client to return as soon as practical following the in vivo trial, in order to review the effort.
The facilitator should reward whatever degree of success the person experiences, and offer continued assistance, with emphasis on self-management skills.
Facilitator: Remember to keep a record in your log of how it goes, what he says, what you say, your thoughts, your feelings and so on. Then come in as soon as you can after it is over, so we can review how you did.
Client: O.K.

Slow and Steady Wins the Race
The client's initial attempts at being assertive should be chosen for their high potential of success, to provide early reinforcement. The more success one has with beginning assertions, the more one is encouraged to keep trying. In addition, each report to the facilitator of a successful assertion obtains added reinforcement. The facilitator must be capable of providing verbal reinforcement for each successful assertive act, and of helping the trainee to develop self-reinforcing thoughts.

Initially then, the individual should begin with small assertions that are likely to be successful and rewarded, and from there proceed to more difficult assertions. Ideally each step should be explored with the facilitator until the client-trainee is capable of being fully in control of most situations. She should be warned against taking initiative to attempt a difficult assertion at first without special preparation. The facilitator also should particularly beware of instigating an assertion where the trainee is likely to fail, thus inhibiting further attempts at assertiveness.

If the trainee does suffer a setback, which very well may happen, the facilitator must be ready to help analyze the situation and rebuild confidence. Especially in the early stages, trainees are prone to mistakes either of inadequate technique or of overzealousness to the point of aggression. Either miscue could cause negative returns, particularly if the "receiver" of the action becomes hostile and/or highly aggressive. The facilitator must be prepared to serve as a buffer and to help re-establish motivation.

Most trainees will have more than one specific problem with being assertive. In the above case, for example, the woman may have difficulty returning items to a store or gaining her rights with roommates. The same basic process with variations may be used for each situation. The individuality of each client must always be accommodated. Provide a learning environment in which trainees may grow in assertiveness, and carefully avoid "shoving it down their throats."

Homework

Assign regular homework which is appropriate to the client's situation. Specific *components* of behavior may be assigned for special practice, such as fluency, posture, listening. In the case of the young woman above, working with a tape recorder on her vocal qualities might be suggested. For some, a mirror may be used to work on eye contact, gestures, and facial expression. Other appropriate homework assignments are geared to specific *situations*, such as starting a conversation with a stranger, returning a faulty item to a store, and — as the trainee gains skills — more difficult situations, such as confronting one's spouse.

Preparation for "Life After AT"

Long before the end of an assertiveness training process (perhaps ranging from several weeks to several months duration) the facilitator must point out important factors for the future. Conscious practice in real-life situations is suggested for at least six months after training. We also encourage clients to re-read *Your Perfect Right* as often as needed to provide continuing motivation and support for assertive ventures.

A key factor in establishing a lasting, independent behavior pattern is to help the trainee understand the need for on-going self-reinforcement. To maintain their newly-developed assertive skills, trainees will need support within their own immediate living environments. Regular feedback from the facilitator will not be available after the training, so "graduates" must arrange for their own rewards for assertiveness, from themselves or other sources close at hand in their lives.

Preparation for the client's independent functioning must begin early in the process of the training.

26

GROUP TRAINING PROCEDURES

When the first edition of *Your Perfect Right* was published in 1970, little work had been done on assertiveness training in groups. Since that time the group has become the "treatment of choice" for most social skills and assertiveness training. For many trainees, the process of assertive behavior development in a group setting is more effective than one-to-one, in part because of the expanded potential for interaction with others during the training process.

Several specific advantages result from a small group. Social skills trainees have typically encountered great anxiety in life situations which involve confronting other people. A group provides a "laboratory" of other people with whom to work — people who share similar problems, needs, and goals. Each member is less alone. The group offers a social environment in which each trainee can be accepted, understood, supported — and therefore comfortable enough to experiment with new behavior.

With several individuals undertaking assertiveness training together, there is a broader base for social modeling. Each trainee sees several others learning to act assertively, and each is able to learn from the strengths and weaknesses of the others.

A group provides more diverse perspectives for feedback than can an individual facilitator. Hearing reactions from several different persons, especially from peers who have nothing to lose from honesty, can speed the behavior-shaping process for each trainee.

Social situations involving a number of people are a frequent source of anxiety. Work in a group gives a realistic opportunity to face several people and overcome that difficulty in a relatively safe training environment.

The group is, of course, a powerful source of social reinforcement for each of its members. Knowing several others are "expecting" one's growth and active effort toward new skills, each member may be stimulated to greater achievement than when working alone. And, for its part, the group rewards new assertiveness with all the force of its social approval. (This asset can become a liability at the *end* of a group unless the trainer has taken steps to develop independence in the trainees.)

In the use of the small group setting for assertiveness and social skills training, it is important to recognize that some trainees are not ready for a group experience. Assessment of individual clients before assignment to a group is the ideal way to address this problem. The assessment would include formal measures and an interview. In Chapter 3 we mentioned several behavioral types to consider screening out. You might wish to refresh your memory by reviewing that list now.

Time considerations may pre-empt conducting a thorough screening. If so, the decision can be made after the fact by observing which clients are not functioning adequately in the group setting. We will ask the person to come and see us individually, at which time a more thorough exploration of the needs and capacities for group work is undertaken. Often the client will voluntarily decide to cease group membership. If not, the group leader needs to make an assertive decision. Preparation of the group for working effectively together will depend upon the setting, the skill and attitudes of the facilitator, and the readiness of group members to respond openly and honestly to one another. Because a discussion of the process of personal interaction in groups is beyond the scope of this book, the interested reader is referred to Yalom (1975), Houts and Serber (1972), and Corey and Corey (1982).

It has been our experience with assertive behavior groups that an atmosphere of trust and concern by group members for one another will grow out of the training process, and that growth toward common objectives will provide the cohesiveness necessary to develop an effective working group. The facilitator, acting as model and guide, sets the tone, and by example encourages trust, support and positive regard for each member of the group.

The Makeup and Format of Training Groups

Numbers. The typical AT/SST group has from five to twelve members. Workshops or classes with greater numbers are not unusual, however the format is necessarily more didactic and less individualized. Fewer than five restricts the potential for social modeling, limits the sources of feedback, and fails to provide the range of behavior styles needed for each trainee to experience a variety of others as each tries out new assertive behaviors. Group work specialists suggest eight as an optimum size; that number works well in social skills training.

Sexes. We prefer, when possible, to balance the number of men and women in our groups, since social relationships with the opposite sex are a frequent source of anxiety for our nonassertive and aggressive clients. A group with equal numbers of each sex has enhanced opportunity for helping its members to deal effectively with social situations involving the opposite sex. We recognize that much work has been done with same-sex groups, particularly for women. There is value in such programs, but our preference is to create a more nearly representative microcosm of the "real world." For some clients, however, work in a same-sex group may be a desirable prerequisite to a mixed group.

Time. Because much social skills training has been developed in university settings, groups are often designed to coincide with the academic term. It is typical for groups to meet one hour twice each week for eight to twelve weeks — a total of sixteen to twenty-four hours.

We have experimented with alternatives, including a format of 10 or 12 one-hour sessions over five or six weeks, then no meetings for approximately three weeks, reconvening again for a follow-up session or two. This approach can be nearly as successful as a longer group. The basic concepts of assertion can be covered and practiced within this short period of time. Motivation tends to remain high for both facilitator and members; absenteeism is reduced. The break encourages members to try out their new learning without regular group support — perhaps more of a "real world" experience — and to identify any major obstacles which may need more attention. If necessary, further work with assertion on a one-to-one basis can be arranged. In selected cases additional therapeutic measures may also be needed.

Two-hours-once-a-week is another schedule which can work. The advantage here is a longer and often more intensive session, but the long interval between sessions seems to be a significant loss to the behavior shaping process.

One study (Berah, 1981) suggests that massed and distributed training formats are equally effective. Brief introductory groups as short as eight one-hour sessions have also been conducted with some success, particularly for those clients who primarily are in need of enhanced awareness of the potential of assertiveness (i.e. "consciousness raising").

Given a choice, we prefer groups of one-and-one-half hours, meeting twice each week for eight to ten weeks. An hour and a half allows time for the balance of didactic and experiential activities desirable in an AT/SST group. And ten weeks is probably as long as most trainees will find the group's feedback and support to be of significant value. We have not conducted formal evaluation of various formats, however, and our preference for this schedule is just that — a personal preference. Trainee needs and the goals for which the training is offered should be the primary determinants of appropriate scheduling.

Trainers. Groups led by co-facilitators are, in our experience, more effective environments for client growth than those led by individual facilitators. Attrition is lower, enthusiasm higher, and both self-report and facilitator observation of growth are greater. We have worked with each other, other psychologists, university staff counselors, and M.A.-level counselor-trainees. Co-facilitators are most effective when they are open and honest with each other and with group members, possess complementary skills and facilitation styles, and are both openly enthusiastic about the training process. In addition, although we have been consistently most effective in assertive groups when working together, we encourage a male-female co-facilitator team. Effective models of both sexes are valuable resources for social skills groups.

The Assertiveness Training Process in Groups

The following material is based on our own style of training, and describes the more or less "typical" procedure we follow in conducting an assertiveness/social skills training group in a therapeutic environment (eg. private practice, university counseling center, outpatient mental health clinic). There are, of course, a wide variety of settings and approaches to training, and the literature contains many descriptions of other methods. Adaptation to the needs of trainees, the setting, and the style of the trainer is a key to the success of any such intervention.

First Session. The initial meeting of our training groups goes something like this: (1) introductory statement on assertive behavior training, (2) getting acquainted exercise, (3) brief demonstration of behavior rehearsal (4) didactic presentation on cognitive issues, (5) homework assignment, and (6) relaxation exercise.

• A ten- to fifteen-minute *introductory statement* on the special nature of this group includes discussion of the non-assertive-aggressive-assertive paradigm described in *Your Perfect Right.* Emphasis is placed on the contributions of behavior, attitudes, and obstacles, in the learning process, and on the situational nature of assertiveness and other social skills. Members are cautioned that assertiveness training is not a panacea, and that they will not discover miraculous changes overnight. They are also told that occasional failure is to be expected, but will not stop long-term progress. Several examples are presented to illustrate why assertive self-expression is to be preferred to the alternatives.

The presentation is concluded with a discussion about how the group will be structured and the kind of exercises which will be presented, along with a "pep talk" about becoming thoroughly involved in changing, the need for risk-taking, and the proven effectiveness of the procedures. Strong emphasis is placed on the importance of individual practice and the support of the group.

Throughout the presentation, we encourage the participants to ask questions, although it can be difficult to get a group of individuals who have difficulty with self-expression to initiate questions, especially at this early stage of the group.

• *Getting acquainted* follows these preliminaries. We use the time-tested "go-around," treating this initial participation exercise as a demonstration of the process to be used in the group. The trainer asks members to close their eyes and visualize themselves completing a brief self-introduction; then the trainer models a one- or two-minute self-introduction, emphasizing personal background and reasons for participating in the group. The imagery step is then repeated, with the suggestion that trainees visualize a "successful" outcome this time.

The introductions exercise represents the first overt group activity to confront the members. For some, of course, considerable anxiety attends this moment. Trainer sensitivity is important here. The introductions must be seen as a natural activity, not a "performance." No one will be "judged." No rules apply, and there are no expectations to live up to. The length and detail of each introduction is strictly a matter of personal choice by the members. Any feedback which comes up in the discussion which follows should be in the nature of positive reinforcement for success.

In the follow-up discussion after the introductions, it can be helpful to inquire about individual thoughts and feelings during the introductions. Most participants will have similar reactions, and the shared impressions will help produce a sense of cohesiveness and identification with the group. At this time the trainer can inform the group that they have just completed the first group exercise, and that the process will be similar in future meetings, although the content will vary, of course.

• A *behavior rehearsal demonstration* is the heart of the first group session. Here the trainer presents a short common scene, then role-plays a brief segment to demonstrate the non-assertive, aggressive, and assertive styles. Members are asked to watch for specific components of behavior (see Chapter 6), and to offer feedback on the trainer's effectiveness in each style. It can be helpful to assign separate components to each trainee, to make feedback more specific.

If training is being conducted with individuals who are functioning relatively well at the outset (i.e. supervisory training rather than assertive behavior therapy), group members may be asked to participate in the first demonstration role-play. However trainers are cautioned not to force or embarrass members into participation at this early stage.

• The first *cognitive presentation* to the group is a mini-lecture on cognitive restructuring, the process of helping individuals to change their thinking about themselves and their attitudes toward acting assertively. Following the modeling demonstration, group members inevitably have a host of rationalizations about "why it will not work well" in their lives. The reaction offers an ideal training opportunity for presenting the cognitive component. A brief introduction to the concept of positive self-statements (see Chapter 9 of *Your Perfect Right*, and Meichenbaum, 1977), is all there is usually time for in the first meeting. As a homework assignment, however, trainees may be asked to write down the negative self-statements they associate with introducing themselves, and to counter each with an opposite positive statement (see "Homework" below).

Our approach to cognitive variables is threefold: (1) mini-lectures and discussions about cognitions based on the material of Meichenbaum, Ellis, Beck, and others; (2) hand-outs and reading assignments relating to the importance of dealing with one's thoughts; (3) on-going monitoring of negative and positive cognitive statements that arise naturally as the group works on assertiveness situations, reviews homework, and discusses real-life problems.

(The cognitive discussion may be put off until the second meeting if time is short.)

• *Homework* is assigned to the trainees as the first session comes to a close, in the form of an ongoing log of their progress, emphasizing specific, detailed examples. They are asked to begin their logs (see Chapter 3 of *Your Perfect Right*) by writing down specific behaviors (within the nonassertive-aggressive-assertive framework) which they wish to change. If time has permitted the cognitive discussion noted above, the self-statements assignment is included as well.

A brief *relaxation exercise* is a good way to end the first group meeting, because anxiety is a major component of the obstacle system for many trainees. Group members are asked to keep track of sources of anxiety in their personal logs between sessions. If anxiety is a significant problem for many group members, it may be necessary to devote a session to anxiety management, or perhaps regularly to include stress inoculation and/or desensitization procedures in group sessions.

Keep in mind that social skills training is not a broad spectrum or holistic treatment. While basic material on cognitions and anxiety is presented, certain participants may need more in-depth individual work which is beyond the scope of the skills training group.

Remember too, that the description above is for a "mainstream" assertiveness training group. Specific procedures in any given setting must account for the unique needs of the trainees. Individuals involved in an on-going individual or group therapy program, as in-patients or out-patients, must be carefully assessed before assignment to assertiveness or social skills training, and their training will usually be geared to basic skills and anxiety reduction. For a group of middle managers in industry, where the main goal may be to improve skills needed to effectively supervise employees, a very different set of priorities and procedures will prevail.

Additional Meetings. A format similar to that of the first group meeting is followed throughout the life of the group, although the emphasis should move from didactic presentations to behavior rehearsal and other experiential elements. Each session is divided roughly thus:
— followup on the homework completed by each individual member;
— didactic presentation of the "cognitive message" for the session;
— practice of skills in a specific situation;
— anxiety management exercises, where indicated by the needs of members;
— assignment of homework for the time between sessions.

• *Homework followup* generally consists of inviting each member to describe his/her experiences with assertion since the last meeting, with specific emphasis on the homework exercise. Homework assignments are an extension of the exercises practiced in the group, to facilitate skill development and transfer to "real world" settings.

• *Didactic presentations* are scheduled to emphasize important aspects of the "philosophy" of assertiveness, and to present ideas for expanding the assertive repertoire of participants. Time is devoted to member questions about concepts, but it is important to avoid trying to counter all the "Yes, but..." resistances you will find among group members. You simply cannot answer all they can come up with, and you will waste a lot of group time trying!

• *Skills practice* remains the heart of AT/SST. Trainees learn more from doing than from talking about doing, almost universally. (Those who are more cognitively oriented do gain much from verbal instruction, of course.) The practice format is like that described for the *introductions* exercise in the opening session: a situation is posed; members are asked to fantasize their individual responses; a model (often but not always the facilitator) role-plays the scene; the group briefly

discusses the model's performance; individual ₁
statements are developed; a new covert respons
cessful outcome) is called for; each member pı~~.~~ and
receives feedback. The major facilitative elements of social
skills training (covert rehearsal, modeling, cognitive restructuring, and skill practice) are built into the group process for
each situation covered.

Following this pattern, we have found it useful to structure the first few weeks of group meetings so that each
member participates in several fundamental exercises such
as (not necessarily in this order):

1. Breaking into a small group of strangers already
engaged in conversation at a party.
2. Starting and maintaining a conversation with a
stranger in a classroom, on a bus, at a meeting.
3. Returning faulty or defective items to a store.
4. Assertiveness with significant others: parents,
roommates, co-workers, bosses, lovers.
5. Saying "no" to a request for a favor.
6. Expressing anger assertively.
7. Asking for a date/refusing a date (telephone and
face-to-face).
8. Expressing compliments; caring feelings; "soft
assertions."
9. Public speaking (2-3 minutes on a favorite topic).
10. Arguing or standing up for oneself with a dominant,
dogmatic, and/or opinionated person.

We operate with considerable flexibility, and may leave
out some situations or add others, according to the apparent
needs of members of a particular group.

Our training agenda emphasizes a full range of assertive
attitudes and behaviors, cutting across particular situations.
More focused approaches for one particular problem, such as
job interviewing, date initiation skills, and conversational

skills, have been reported in the literature. (For a comprehensive analysis of group social skills training see Kelly, 1985).

After all group members have completed the basic exercises, they are encouraged to bring to the group current life situations which are troubling them. At this point individual situations presented in the group frequently relate to intimate relationships: "How can I tell my father to stop nagging me? How can I tell my boyfriend that I don't really love him? My roommate has terrible B.O! My boss keeps making passes at me. I yell at my wife and children every day when I get home from work. No one pays any attention to me."

Although no one is denied the opportunity to present a personal situation earlier in the group process, most participants are reluctant to expose much of themselves very early in the life of the group. Some trainers choose to invite members to present "real life" situations from the beginning of a group. Our experience has been that some will be too anxious and may be threatened if the material is individualized too early. Thus it is usually more valuable to structure the first meetings, and move toward member-initiated activities after the facilitation process is well established, and participants have come to trust one another more fully.

Very personal situations are more sensitive and difficult to handle than the "clerk-in-the-store" variety, since they involve on-going relationships with great emotional investment. Sensitivity, patience, and careful attention to the principles of assertiveness — and to the consideration of consequences — are in order here, and the facilitator is cautioned against pat solutions to unique individual problems. Under these conditions other members of a perceptive and caring group are often the most valuable resource to the facilitator. Rehearsing approaches to significant others is usually very worthwhile in the group, if only to gain a better understanding of one's own feelings about the person/

situation. It is a rare group which does not offer support and caring in delicate situations.

Practice in the expression of caring for another is, of course, an important goal of a social skills training group. (Chapter 12 of *Your Perfect Right* discusses the "soft assertions" in some detail.) We focus considerable attention upon the verbal expression of positive feelings toward oneself and others.

Similarly, at another point in the emotional spectrum, putting angry feelings into words is an important group exercise. We encourage group members to practice assertive anger expression (review Chapters 13 and 27).

• *Homework assignments* are based upon the group's needs at the end of each session, and with some awareness of progress toward the stated goals (including those unique to this group, both from the pre-group assessment and from member statements at the first meeting). Most homework is practice of assertive and cognitive skills learned in the group. Anxiety management exercises are also valuable, as are written assignments in the personal log. (Maintaining the log is an ongoing homework assignment.)

Often individual members will be asked to follow through on a personal situation which they have presented to the group and practiced during a session. Each member will be expected to report on the assignment at the following meeting. A "buddy system," which pairs group members to support and encourage the completion of homework, can be a very helpful device (Shelton and Ackerman, 1974).

• *Translating to the "real world."* As the assertive behavior group passes the middle of its schedule, we urge the members to sensitize themselves to sources of continuing reinforcement for assertion in their individual life environments. The group is an important center of support for the developing assertiveness of each member. However, it will come to an end, and trainees must take responsibility for identifying and expanding sources of support within their own "ecosystems." Internal positive thoughts and self-statements are a key to this step.

The final meeting of our assertiveness training groups is usually devoted to a very uplifting emotional experience developed by psychologist Herbert Otto (1969): the "Strength Bombardment." Members of the group are given approximately one minute each to speak about themselves in only *positive* terms — no qualifiers, no criticisms, no "buts." Immediately thereafter, the rest of the group gives to each member an additional two minutes of *positive* feedback. The time may be varied to suit the group, but caution is urged: don't allow enough for embarrassing — and painful — silence. The "clockwatcher" can be flexible, but the important note is that this must be a positive experience for *each* member. The facilitator needs to be prepared to fill any gaps in the feedback portion for the most "unlovable" group member, and to encourage the too-modest reluctant starter. The facilitator is encouraged to be the first speaker in this exercise, as a model of self-assertion and to demonstrate appropriate positive statements to make about oneself.

On Improving Feedback in Groups

One of the important values of using a group format is the diversity of viewpoints available for providing feedback to participants on the effectiveness of their self-expressions. Nevertheless, many group members find it difficult to give good feedback, and it is useful to spend some time training a group in how the members can best help each other.

Toward that goal, it is suggested that the qualities of good interpersonal feedback be pointed out to the group. The following list identifies a number of characteristics.

Helpful feedback:

...describes *specific* verbal and non-verbal behaviors in detail;

...avoids telling "how *I* would do it";

...focuses on the *behavior*, not the *person*;

...gives *observations* and *descriptions*, not *opinions* and *judgements*;

...is for the benefit of the *receiver*, not the *giver*;

...gives *information*, not *instructions*, thus allowing the trainee to choose what he or she will do with the information.

One additional comment about feedback which may be of interest. A number of groups have utilized poker chips as tokens, encouraging group members to toss a chip at the feet of a member to indicate — by chip color — whether a particular action was assertive, nonassertive, or aggressive. The immediacy of such feedback is valuable, and the chips themselves create a novel source of group interest (and fun!). However, such global feedback needs to be supplemented with specifics about behavior as soon afterward as possible, in order to be of maximum value in aiding the development of more effective behavior.

• *Coaching Triads* is a rehearsal and feedback approach we have found valuable in our groups. Instead of pairing off, the group is divided into sets of three, with one member practicing an appropriate response to the situation ("sender"), a second member playing the role of spouse, clerk in the store, boss, etc. ("receiver"), and the third observing and giving feedback. Each person takes a turn in each role. The triads provide a better feedback system than pairs, since the feedback is given to both participants in the rehearsal, and the observer has no other function but observation and feedback. In addition, by rotating, all have the opportunity to gain perspective in handling a wide range of behaviors.

Other Formats for Social Skills and Assertiveness Training

We have described in considerable detail an approach to

group facilitation which has worked well for us over a period of years. Our style has modified, of course, as we have found new and better means for achieving the goals of our group participants. Nevertheless, we are under no illusion that there is only one way to conduct effective assertiveness/social skills training groups. We know that many of our colleagues find other styles more appropriate in their own group work, some with more structure, some with less, some more rigorous in application of learning principles, others with a greater humanistic-existential flavor.

Although we have no quarrel with these and other approaches to the development of effective social behavior, we remain convinced that application of the principles detailed in this book will enable clients to achieve their behavioral goals. And that, of course, is the ultimate criterion.

The wide range of interests of practitioners, researchers, and theorists has led to the development of a variety of approaches to meet special needs and to suit the styles of the professionals involved. We consider this diversity very healthy since the resulting training process has been enriched by a relatively free exchange of ideas and discoveries.

Social skills training is, as L'Abate (1985) has observed, "one of the most widely deployed intervention strategies for the delivery of mental health services." That has resulted, at least in part, because it has not been limited by rigid adherence to "rules" established by a "founding guru."

We have benefitted from the excellent work of many colleagues around the world who have helped to develop effective AT/SST procedures. The following material is a very brief overview of some important contributions to AT. Space and time make a fully comprehensive review impractical. Refer often to the sources cited, in the process of developing and refining your own style.

General Concepts

Four social myths which are responsible for much non-assertive behavior have been described by *Sherwin Cotler* and *Julio Guerra* (1976). The myths of *anxiety, obligation, modesty,* and the *good friend* help to explain much of the belief system which inhibits self-assertion as it is defined by the popular (pre-AT) culture. Understanding of the false premises inherent in these myths does much to free trainees to attempt assertions.

AT as a part of the broader framework of behavior therapy has been a theme of *Herbert Fensterheim* (1975), and *Spencer Rathus* (1978). Their work has focused attention on the need to view the clinical client in a broad therapeutic framework, with emphasis on anxiety reduction as well as assertion skills training. Fensterheim has also identified a several "clinical problem types" which are amenable to AT treatment.

Cognitive restructuring, the process of aiding clients to change their self-defeating thoughts, beliefs, and attitudes, was advocated in early popular treatises by *Iris Fodor* and *Janet Wolfe* (1975), and *Arthur Lange* and *Patricia Jakubowski* (1976). They have developed (independent but complementary) systems for helping clients to overcome faulty belief systems and to gain more positive and rational conceptions of their life situations. Much of their work has integrated the work of *Donald Meichenbaum* (1977) in cognitive behavior therapy and the Rational Emotive Therapy of *Albert Ellis* (1979, 1980) with AT. Moreover, they have been outspoken advocates of *responsibility* as an element of assertiveness, and high ethical standards for facilitators.

These significant works in the cognitive behavioral realm, along with those of of *Aaron Beck* (1979), *Gary Emery* (1984), and others, has led to major changes in the procedures of many behavioral techniques. Assertiveness and social skills training now includes considerable emphasis on the cognitive elements (c.f. Dodson, 1988 and Freeman, et al., 1989).

Innovative Procedures

Scripts, and a procedure for developing your own assertive messages, is a central feature of the work of *Sharon Bower* (1976). She offers scripts for specific life events, and a general formula (*D*escribe behavior; *E*xpress feelings; *S*pecify desired change; Identify *C*onsequences) for preparing scripts to meet any situation. Her procedures are very systematic and highly detailed.

Cultural differences have been taken into consideration by only a few AT practitioners or writers. *Donald Cheek* (1976) offers a thorough analysis of cultural considerations in AT. His material examines the effect on behavior of the psycho-social history of a group (specifically Blacks in America), and presents a new AT methodology designed to accommodate the special needs of Black clients. Of particular note are his emphasis on *language barriers* between black and white, and his concern for adapting the assertive message to the *target person.*

Other important contributors to multicultural AT include those of *Brian Grodner* (1977), *Philip Hwang* (1977), *Paula Landau* and *Terry Paulson* (1977), and *Evelyn Yanagida* (1979).

Assessment instruments in AT are plentiful (See Chapter 22). Thoroughly researched instruments, however, are few. *Merna* and *John Galassi* (1977) have been active researchers and practitioners in AT, and have studied assessment devices extensively, including development of their own college and adult "Self Expression Scales." Moreover, they offer a method for devising an individualized assessment scale tailored to the needs of each trainee. They also were leaders in the move to establish ethical principles for AT practice. See also *Peter Vagg* (1979).

Among other widely used AT measures are the *Rathus Assertiveness Schedule,* by *Spencer Rathus* (1973), and the *Assertion Inventory* by *Eileen Gambrill* and *Cheryl Richey*

(1975). The *Interpersonal Behavior Survey* by *Paul Mauger*, et al. (1980) impressed us, and has in recent years become something of a standard.

Sherwin Cotler and *Julio Guerra* (1976) assembled one of the most comprehensive data collection packages for use in AT, including anxiety measures, assertiveness scales, goal surveys and homework diaries. They emphasized systematic monitoring of trainee anxiety through use of the numerical "Subjective Unit of Disturbance" scale first presented by *Joseph Wolpe* (See Chapter 9 of *Your Perfect Right*).

The "personal effectiveness" skills training program (which parallels AT), developed by *Robert Liberman* and his associates (1976), includes a group procedure which calls for planning, work, and evaluation sessions, so that time is clearly provided for each of those three group tasks.

Specific Techniques

Many techniques have been effectively utilized by AT practitioners and are worthy of mention here. Although we have noted, in the brief summaries below, names of professionals whom we associate with the development of a particular procedure, the exact origin of many techniques is unknown or simultaneous, and we make no claim for the accuracy of our attributions.

Homework Assignments take AT from the training environment into the "life space" of the trainee. Responsible and appropriate assignments are those which would be natural to the client's lifestyle, and would not demand that he or she behave in an embarrassing, highly unusual or bizarre fashion. *John Shelton* (1974) has been a major developer of systematic homework in AT and other forms of therapy.

Contrasted Role Plays, an insight-oriented model for role playing in AT groups, is the work of *Linda MacNeilage* and *Kathleen Adams* (1977). The model incorporates a Gestalt notion of "reconciliation of opposites" by having the trainee enact three contrasting responses to a situation (unassertive, aggressive, assertive), thus experiencing the full range of emotional and behavioral alternatives.

Verbal Techniques have been widespread and take many forms. The DESC scripts of *Sharon Bower* (see "Innovative Procedures" above) are a very precise guide to assertive language. *Myles Cooley* and *James Hollandsworth* (1977) devised a "components" strategy for teaching assertive statements, classified in three general areas: saying "no" or taking a stand (position, reason, understanding); asking favors or asserting rights (problem, request, clarification); and expressing feelings (personal expression).

Among the "last resort" techniques used by some trainers are the "broken record," "fog," "selective ignoring," and "critical inquiry," (*Cotler* and *Guerra, 1976*). Each of these is an effort to overcome unfair manipulation or attack, and are considered appropriate only when the trainee has decided that the possible consequence of ending the relationship is worth risking. Briefly, "broken record" involves repetitive expressions of one's position; "fog" is a passive-aggressive agreement with the other person ("Whatever you say, dear"); "selective ignoring" is withholding any response when one feels the other is being unreasonable, unfair, or aggressive; "critical inquiry" is an invitation to the critical person to *be* even more critical, and thus emphasize undesired behavior. Once learned, of course, these techniques may be *used* aggressively and not just in self-defense. Cotler and Guerra are careful to point out the dangers in these "last resort" approaches, and do not advocate their general use (nor do *we*, needless to say!).

27

FACILITATING ASSERTIVE ANGER EXPRESSION

Everybody has an idea about anger. And every human service professional has a pet theory about how to deal with it. There are ventilationists, analysts, rationalists, behaviorists... everybody is an "expert"!

Not to be outdone, we have developed our own approach for working with anger expression in the context of assertiveness and social skills training. We claim no magic, but we believe these methods are based on the most enlightened thinking on the subject. (In other words, we *like* these ideas!) We've avoided such popular notions as venting, pillow pounding, and "you create your own reality," in favor of such straightforward procedures as cognitive restructuring, behavior rehearsal, and relaxation training.

Anger expression is such a key element of assertiveness training that we urge you to re-read Chapter 14 of *Your Perfect Right*, so you'll recall our basic views on the subject, before you proceed with this chapter.

Theoretically...

Let's take a short walk through the common theoretical views of anger and aggression. So many folks seem to believe that we humans are aggressive animals by nature, and that angry behavior just naturally follows from that. Is it true? We don't think so, and — according to the "Seville Statement" (see Chapter 14) — the weight of scientific opinion agrees with us.

The Myth of "Instinctive Aggression"

"Look at the history of humankind," you say, "wars, violence, inhumanity, street fights, child abuse, senseless killings. I *must* believe that we are *naturally* aggressive beings." Nope. But our social systems do tend to give a great deal of reinforcement for "aggression" even in its less violent forms: the "aggressive" salesperson, the "highly competitive" athlete, the "hard-nosed" manager, the "strong-willed" politician — all tend to be esteemed.

Popular views of the "aggression-is-natural" viewpoint include those of such heavyweights as psychoanalyst Sigmund Freud, ethologist Konrad Lorenz, and psychotherapist George Bach. They offer persuasive arguments:

Freud: "The tendency to aggression is an innate, independent, instinctual disposition in man."

(*Civilization and Its Discontents,* Chapter 6).

Lorenz: "We find that aggression...is really an essential part of the life-preserving organization of instincts."

(*On Aggression*, page 44).

George Bach: "The healthy fusion of aggression with developmental process is crucial to the child's eventual mastery of the environment and his struggle for survival in a difficult, competitive culture."

(*Creative Aggression,* page 45).

Can we dismiss our disagreement with these views as merely an honest difference of opinion? No. The most enlightened evidence supports a view of aggression as a *potential, but not universal* form of behavior. It would be foolish to deny the widespread existence of human aggression, but good cross-cultural studies show that it is not a universal form of human expression.

It is worth noting again: *aggression* is not the same thing as *anger!* Anger is a perfectly natural, healthy human emotion which may be expressed in a number of ways, including aggressively, nonassertively, assertively, or not at all. Anger is a *feeling,* an emotion we all feel at times. Aggression is a *behavioral style* of expression.

Simplistic, "instinctive" theories of aggression are no longer viable, if indeed they ever were. Ethologists like Lorenz, aided by popular writers such as Robert Ardrey (1966), presented a view of instinctive human aggressive behavior which, like the animal cousins we were said to emulate, appeared whenever we were called upon to defend honor, life, or territory. Lorenz further advocated the regular release of our aggressive energy, lest it "build up" and come out spontaneously in uncontrolled, potentially destructive ways (and contributing, along with Sigmund Freud, to widespread misunderstanding of how anger really works in the human organism).

Paralleling the work of Lorenz, an entire school of psychotherapy grew up around the notion of "letting it out," integrating Freudian concepts of the innate need to express energy with Gestalt notions of the oneness of mind and body and existential philosophy of living each moment "in the here-and-now." Therapists Fritz Perls, George Bach and a host of their followers got clients up off the couch, shouting at each other in groups, flailing each other with foam bats and epithets, confronting feelings loudly, and expressing aggression "creatively." (We tried it, too, until we learned better.)

The notion of a natural human need to express emotion is attractive — we like it too. And while there may be some value in "venting" strong feelings, that's *not* the way to help folks learn to express their anger.

The clear evidence from the most careful experimental studies is that *aggression produces aggression.* Thus, if you learn — as a young child under your parents' tutelage, or as an adult taught by a therapist — to express strong feelings aggressively (hurtfully), you will adopt an aggressive style. Under stress, we tend to fall back on our old, well-learned habits. (Remember the Uvaldo Palomares story in Chapter 24?)

Psychologist Leonard Berkowitz (1965, 1969) reported classic experimental studies which confirm that there are nonviolent methods of emotional release which contain the benefits but not the harmful effects of direct aggression. He suggests that a direct aggressive attack provokes additional aggression, both in the attacker and in the subject.

In one study, for instance, women who were insulted were permitted two styles of response. Group one was allowed to describe their angry feelings to the insulter (e.g., "That really makes me mad"). Group two women were given freedom to strike back and attack the insulter. After the experiment, the women who *described* their feelings (group one) maintained less hostile feelings toward their insulter than did the women in group two, who were permitted to *attack* directly.

Berkowitz and other psychologists who have studied aggressive social interaction conclude, from the results of many such studies, that although individuals may "feel better" after venting hostility aggressively, such reinforcement of destructive acts leads to further hurtful behavior. (See Tavris, 1982, and McKay et al., 1989).

We agree with these findings, and believe assertiveness training offers a particularly appropriate format for learning effective and nondestructive forms of anger expression.

Assertive responses can both effectively express strong feelings *and* give the other person a chance to respond non-defensively — perhaps even to change that behavior which resulted in anger in the first place.

As research and more sophisticated analyses of human behavior have evolved, the position of *social learning theory* most adequately explains the nature of aggressive — and other — behavior. Albert Bandura, leading theorist of the social learning viewpoint states it succinctly (1973):

The social learning theory of human aggression adopts the position that man is endowed with neurophysiological mechanisms that enable him to behave aggressively, but the activation of these mechanisms depends upon appropriate stimulation and is subject to cortical control. Therefore, the specific forms that aggressive behavior takes, the frequency with which it is expressed, the situations in which it is displayed, and the specific targets elected for attack are largely determined by social experience. (pp. 29-30)

Thus, in a refinement of the "instinct" notion, contemporary theorists of the social learning and socio-biology schools agree that humans have the genetic *potential* which makes aggression *possible* — but not automatic or universal. *Social and cultural learning* determines how a person will respond under particular circumstances, and governs one's personal standards for the appropriateness of particular actions.

Humans have the power of conscious choice as to whether, when, and how to express anger. Needless to say, we advocate the assertive alternative!

A "Synthetic" Model of Anger Expression

Robert Alberti has developed a model for examining anger which combines the theoretical position we have endorsed with the chronology of an anger event in four stages. He refers to it as a "synthetic" model, since it represents a *synthesis* of theory, research, and practice — and because he hopes it is "flexible" enough to expand as new facts emerge on the subject.

The model is set within the context of the individual's environment, and evolves on a time line extending from the before the anger event, through the four stages, ending afterward. The content of the model focuses on physiological, cognitive, and social variables in the person during the four stages.

As more is learned about the interaction of emotion and cognition, and about the brain's structure and control of behavior, such a simple model will give way to a more complex and comprehensive analysis. For now, however, it represents an improvement over the mythology of anger.

A "SYNTHETIC" MODEL OF ANGER/EMOTION

Environmental Context
(Physical / Political / Economic / Cultural / Social)

Preexisting Person Variables	Event-Related Person Variables	Response Variables	Outcome Variables
Physiological Health Disabilities Fatigue Tension Diet Chemical Balance	*Physiological* Sensations Hypothalamic Emissions Muscle Tonus Reflexive Responses	*Physiological* Speech Muscle Action Integrated Movement Feedback	*Physiological* Tension Relief Movement "Punched Out"
Cognitive Attitudes / Beliefs / Values Intellectual Development Expectations	*Cognitive* Perceptions Appraisals / Evaluations Plans	*Cognitive* Goal(s) Language Directions to Motor System Evaluation of Consequences Timing-Duration Act or Withdraw	*Cognitive* Goals Attained Goal Failure Evaluation Change Attitude / Belief Change Satisfaction
Social Roles Relationships Status	*Social* Specific Relationship Social Reinforcers	*Social* Effect Change	*Social* Context Change Relationship Change Role(s) Change No Change

(EVENT)

→ Time →

Working With Anger Expression in AT

Anger can, of course, be an issue to deal with at any time during your work with a client or group. Because it is such a key issue in assertiveness, however, we believe it should be given a spot of its own in a comprehensive training program with individuals, groups, or workshops.

The topic is introduced with a brief didactic presentation, summarizing the material in Chapter 14 of *Your Perfect Right*. We encourage clients to consider carefully the wide range of possible anger responses, from mild irritation through agitation and fury to blind rage. This helps them to recognize how rarely anger is truly something to be feared, since the extreme is quite unusual for most people. Relaxation practice is integrated into this session as well, since much of the early emphasis is on reducing fears of the "terrible" consequences of expressing anger.

For clients who demonstrate particular difficulty with anger expression, it can be valuable to assign homework in the form of additional readings in preparation for the anger work. Tavris (1982) McKay, Rogers, and McKay (1989), and Hankins (1988) are the resources we consider most useful for this purpose.

Using the behavioral modeling procedure which is a key element throughout an AT/SST program, we demonstrate aggressive, nonassertive, and assertive ways to respond to a mildly irritating situation, such as a friend who arrives late for a planned excursion. It is important, as always, to sensitize trainees to the differences in style of the three responses, as reflected in such components as facial expression, gestures, and voice volume, as well as content.

We invite trainees to begin active participation in their own anger expression training by simply repeating the phrase, "I'm angry about that." At first, the statement may be made softly, with little or no emotion. Then we encourage them to repeat the statement with increasing emphasis on non-verbal component expression, adding appropriately angry facial expression, gestures, voice characteristics, etc. This exercise can be very frightening for some clients, especially those with high generalized anxiety and extreme emotional inhibition. Observe carefully, and don't push anyone too far too fast. Work with high anxiety separately where necessary, or make appropriate referral.

After the introductory consciousness raising exercise, it is helpful to allow trainees to relax a bit while you discuss the four-stage approach to dealing with anger: preparation, coping, action, follow-up (described in Chapter 14). Pay particular attention to helping clients recognize the importance of their own attitudes which "set up" angry reactions, and to the methods they can use (e.g. stress inoculation, relaxation responses) to avoid angry confrontations. While we do not discourage appropriate anger expression, we certainly don't think the world needs any more anger than necessary.

The next anger training procedure is to begin the standard step-by-step behavior rehearsal process, using an anger-inducing situation (perhaps one suggested by a client during the session). Here you'll follow the procedures of Chapters 12 and 25 or 26, as appropriate. Employ the skill training model for as much time as your training format provides, or, for an individual client, for as long as it takes to deal with anger as a life issue.

An important element at this stage, of course, will be the preparation of trainees for the role of *receiver* of anger expression by others. As one or more trainees in a group, for example, are learning and practicing anger expression, others will be hearing and responding to the anger, if you use the behavior rehearsal procedure. The trainer will need to do a great deal of modeling of this role in the early stages.

Some desensitization procedures may also be required, to help particularly fearful clients to be able to listen to increasing levels of anger without high anxiety. It is likely that there will be much laughter in the early stages of anger practice; laughter defuses anger and allows anxious persons to deal with it more comfortably. Nevertheless, for purposes of fostering new learning, it should be discouraged in favor of more direct expression.

In preparation of trainees to deal with each other's anger in practice sessions, refer to the steps noted in Chapter 14, "When Somebody Else Is Angry With You." You may find this a difficult stage of the training. Go slowly, include much relaxation, model often, be persistent but sensitive. Do not force anyone beyond his or her limits. Effective treatment of "anger anxiety" may require therapy outside the AT sessions. Don't expect any dramatic progress in a brief intervention; anger is a complex and powerful emotion.

We like to end an anger-training session with a relaxation exercise. These procedures can be highly stimulating, and it is best to get everyone "calmed down" before they go back to their day-to-day activities.

Throughout this process of anger expression training, it will be necessary to be sensitive to:

... your own ability to deal with anger and its expression;

... the anxiety level of very anxious and/or inhibited trainees;

... possible aggressive acting out by belligerent or potentially sociopathic clients (who should be excluded from AT groups unless in an institutional setting for treating such persons).

Dealing with Aggression in Others

From time to time, you will experience individual clients or group members who are disruptive or actually threatening to you or other trainees. While each such circumstance is unique, there are a few general guidelines which will help you to prepare for and deal with such occasions:

Get Ready. Prepare in advance to deal with such situations, so you are ready when they do occur:
• Acknowledge that this may happen to you, and that you must be prepared.
• Re-read Chapter 17, "Dealing With Difficult People."
• Learn and practice appropriate techniques for stress management.
• Learn and practice appropriate techniques for assertive action.
• Get to know your own anger, what triggers it, and how you can most effectively remain calm under stress.
• Identify back-up resources in the location of your practice, so you can seek help if needed.
• Set clear ground rules for off-limits behavior at the outset of training.

When A Confrontation Occurs. You're prepared, so you can take specific steps to keep on top of the problem:
• Intervene early, before the situation gets out of hand.
• Speak to the disrupter individually, if possible.
• Use self-relaxation.
• Keep your voice calm.
• Don't try to "put down" the aggressor.
• Don't try one-upmanship, or "can you top this?"
• Use the situation as an opportunity to model and practice assertiveness.
• Use a co-facilitator or other back-up system to shunt the aggressor away from the group if necessary.
• Arrange a later meeting, when things have calmed down, and after you've met your obligation to the group.

Anger is one of the toughest elements of an assertiveness training program, for the clients and for the trainer. Prepare yourself well, learn about and deal with your own anger effectively, avoid the myths, proceed slowly and carefully, stay relaxed and in control. It'll go better than you expect.

28

APPLICATIONS OF ASSERTIVENESS TRAINING

Assertiveness training has application in a broad range of human activities. While you can identify the usefulness of AT in your own situation, this chapter describes a variety of settings in which the assertive behavior development process can be important.

Most of the examples suggested here have been drawn from the experiences of the authors, friends, colleagues, and students, or from professional literature. Others will doubtless occur in your own setting. Review the entire list. Keep in mind that, although the settings may vary, the general principles of AT apply in each case — *including the ethical principles* noted in the Appendix.

Teachers. The classroom teacher will frequently find students whose behavior is nonassertive or aggressive.

Assertiveness training is highly valuable for students who wish to become better able to raise questions in class, to make presentations and reports, to respond to teacher questions, to express opinions, or to participate in group discussions. Similarly, AT is pertinent to helping students who seem to "come on too strongly" in asking questions, expressing opinions, and so on.

Joyce and Weil (1986) present assertiveness training as a teaching model. Teachers may employ the model to help students with a wide variety of situations: talking to parents, teachers, and other authorities; dealing with teasing, insults, fighting; refusing unreasonable requests; overcoming shyness. The Joyce-Weil model has five phases: identifying target behaviors; setting priorities; role playing; reenactments; transfer.

An increasing volume of work with young children indicates tremendous potential for pre-school and early elementary age youngsters. A leader in this work is Dr. Pat Palmer, psychologist at the Assertiveness Training Institute of Denver, Colorado, who has written two books on AT for children (1977), and more recently developed an approach for adolescents as well (Palmer and Froehner, 1989).

Teacher Education. Children need to learn assertiveness, and so do their teachers. Among the chief complaints of teachers are difficulty in "handling the kids" (discipline), lack of communication with supervisors, and fear of parent conferences. If a teacher is nonassertive much of the time, the students will typically take advantage of the weakness. On the other hand, an aggressive tyrant will be feared but not respected, counter-productive in the learning environment. Assertive communication — of principles and with principals and parents — is essential for teachers. Teachers must also respect children and parents as people, their equals as human beings, and approach them accordingly.

One faculty group set out to learn assertive techniques for

helping their students and found after a short time that much of their own behavior with administrators, students and parents was nonassertive or aggressive. They began to focus on their own need for assertiveness; the result was a highly enthusiastic report about their own growth in effective personal and professional expression.

A classroom-based program which has gained considerable popularity — and notoriety — is known as "assertive discipline" (Canter, 1976). Many teachers and administrators consider this classroom management program to be highly valuable; others find it unacceptably restrictive. Key issues have recently been aired in the professional literature (Canter, 1988; Curwin, 1988, 1989; Hill, 1990; McCormack, 1989; Render, 1989).

It is our opinion that teachers and student teachers should take part in assertiveness training — preferably based on our model, of course! — as a routine segment of their preparation and inservice training for classroom teaching.

Coaches. Every coach of athletic, music, drama or forensic groups has worked with students of considerable potential who were unwilling to try new behavior or to perform individually (e.g., carry the ball, solo) or, conversely, to be "part of the team." For the reluctant student who wishes to achieve his or her potential in these areas, assertiveness training can be a big help. (Indeed, the principles of behavior shaping have been successfully applied in athletics for years.) Students whose style is usually aggressive can be taught to temper their approach, and to develop behaviors more in line with acceptable norms. Coaches who can channel these abilities by fostering assertion will benefit both the player and the team. Connelly (1988), for example, in writing about issues of nonassertiveness, aggressiveness, and assertiveness in coaching athletes, emphasizes that desired attitudes and actions of athletes should be presented by distinguishing between positive assertive and overly aggressive play.

ᴄounselors. The mental health professional will readily recognize the potential of assertiveness training for clients who demonstrate poor social development, inadequate self-confidence, academic disinterest, inability to withstand peer, parental, or teacher pressure. The indecisive individual who wishes to improve decision-making capacity, the non-dater who lacks rudimentary social skills, the student who fears going to see a teacher to ask legitimate questions about the subject matter, the student who eagerly expresses her- or himself but denies others their opportunity, the person who has made a well-considered decision to leave college but is unable to face parents — all of these and many more need to learn how they can more comfortably express themselves as they wish to. AT/SST can help.

College Student Development Staff. Individuals working in college residence halls, activities-union programs, student health centers, placement offices, special education programs, financial aid offices, minority programs, campus religious programs, and deans' offices have broad daily contact with college students. The perceptive residence hall advisor knows the student who cannot stand up to a roommate to ask relief from the stereo's unreasonable noise level. A would-be student leader who lacks the confidence to campaign for office will be identified by staff members who work with organizations. Medical personnel recognize the rash on a shy student as symptomatic of anxiety over presenting a report in class tomorrow. The placement staff can readily spot in advance the student who will suffer in an upcoming job interview for not knowing how to act in that new and threatening situation. All of these student development staff members are very much aware of the individual who seems to offend others by being too outspoken, brusque or verbally or physically abusive. Because the assertive behavior shaping process is systematic and straightforward, these staff members can be of direct help *on the spot* to the student with such problems. There are obvious advantages to help offered by a *known* person, with little or no delay, without the need to seek out another office and establish a relationship with a new and unknown person.

Therapists. Interpersonal anxiety is a common symptom in persons who have emotional difficulties. Assertiveness training can be a vital factor in reducing this anxiety. The basic principles we have proposed apply, regardless of the setting, be it in correctional work, private therapy practice, substance abuse clinics, recovery programs, or other settings. Persons who lack feelings of self-worth can be helped by facilitating their own development of "worthy person" behaviors (making their own choices, standing up for their rights successfully but nonaggressively). Changing of attitudes and feelings goes hand in hand with changed behavior.

Speech Therapists. Adult stutterers have responded well to AT in conjunction with other techniques of behavior therapy such as systematic desensitization. Stutterers usually have a long history of disfluency beginning in their elementary school years. Often they have been "worried over" by parents and teachers, placed in special education classes for therapy, and teased by their peers. As time goes on they learn very well not to expose themselves to situations where attention will be focused on their speech. These individuals learn to be very nondemanding of others, often subordinating their own rights. They may believe that they are not as good as others, and therefore have no right to be assertive.

Because of their dread of interpersonal situations, individuals with speech difficulties can benefit from AT to overcome or inhibit anxiety. Assertive acts such as use of the telephone, talking to sales clerks, asking questions, learning how to disagree, learning to say no, and so on, can be practiced successfully. Long-established patterns of self-denial and lack of spontaneity can be altered significantly.

Social Workers. The welfare recipient often lives in substandard housing in the least desirable location in a community, suffering the indignities of the welfare system. Assertiveness training can help to increase self-respect, teach more adaptive ways of behaving in conjunction with gaining rights, develop effective community leadership, assist persons in methods for dealing with merchants, insure fair treatment without self-denial or aggressive acts. The frequent use of group work and the practice of family case work provide other opportunities for assertive behavior development in this field.

Inevitable vulnerability to the political system is a particular concern in welfare programs. Assertive community action offers a potential avenue for increasing "clout" and stabilizing fiscal support. (See also "Human Liberation" below.)

Employment Counselors. Efforts to place persons in productive and rewarding employment are greatly enhanced when clients are able to demonstrate self-confidence and to communicate effectively with interviewers and employers. Often a simple rehearsal of interviewing behavior provides a client with the tools and confidence needed to gain an appropriate position. Another person may require more extensive help in building up an improved self-image by developing more effective assertive behaviors. Those who are reinforced for behaving in self-assured ways begin to recognize their own strengths. A client may not be aware of coming across too aggressively, and may need help learning how to modify that approach.

(Chapter 16 of *Your Perfect Right* presents many specific suggestions about work-related assertiveness. See also Mac-Neilage and Adams, 1982, and Bolles, 1990.)

Marriage Counselors. When a couple comes in for marriage counseling it is almost a foregone conclusion that they are not communicating successfully. Three situations are common: the husband has been the dominant decision-maker throughout the marriage with the woman being the dutiful headnodder; the reverse situation, in which the husband is quiet and indecisive, and the wife is dominant; and neither partner is dominant, but neither has really known the other's thoughts and feelings all these years. All three of these situations are responsive to the assertiveness training model. As noted earlier, learning assertiveness will change one's relationship with those closest. For this reason it is preferable to have both partners working on the relationship, but if each spouse is truly assertive, the difficulty will not likely balloon into a major crisis (Lazarus, 1985).

We are convinced that the more honest and open each partner is about all aspects of the marital relationship the more successful that relationship will be. Similarly, families who encourage freedom of expression on the part of children provide more growth-enhancing environments for young persons *and* their parents (Palmer, 1977; Palmer and Froehner, 1989).

Lehman-Olson (1983) has prepared an analysis of the basic background of assertiveness training within marital and family therapy. She points to four implications: assertive behavior provides a means for operationalizing marriage and family goals; assertive behavior can be used to assess therapeutic effectiveness; marriage and family contexts provide unique opportunities for training *in situ* and minimize the disadvantages of *in vivo* training; assertiveness training procedures maximize the opportunity to affect both intrapersonal and interpersonal dynamics.

Pastoral Counselors. One of our clients who had built up fears and doubts about being assertive could still remember from childhood a sign in a Sunday School room: "The formula for *JOY* is: *J*esus first, *O*thers second, *Y*ourself last." Unfortunately, to many youngsters (and oldsters), such messages mean quite pointedly, "don't step out ahead of others," "let others take advantage of you," "turn the other cheek," "keep your feelings inside."

There seems to be an idea among many religious people that they must never feel good about themselves. Because they must never hurt anyone's feelings, they will let others take advantage of them. It is a moot point whether it is religious education which discourages believers from feeling good about themselves or standing up for themselves. The goal is to help these individuals to become self-confident. We feel that clients with religious-based barriers to assertion need re-education about what it truly means to be assertive. There need be no incompatibility between asserting one's perfect (i.e., God-given, natural, inherent) rights and having deep religious convictions.

A number of authors have addressed the area of assertiveness within a religious context. Scot Bolsinger and Mark McMinn (1989) suggest that, although psychotherapists may recognize that values are important in dealing with clients, little attention has been given to *how* they introduce and implement assertiveness training with *religious* clients. Ethan J. Allen, Jr. (1976) discusses the "nice-guy" syndrome, noting that those trained to be priests have a reputation for being cheerful in the face of insult and unassertive when others disregard their rights. Seminarians may be regarded as the classic "Caspar Milquetoast." Randy K. Sanders (1976) speaks of a theologically oriented approach to assertiveness training, overcoming misconceptions about such behavior as passively "turning the other cheek." Sanders suggests that a religious AT facilitator may need to teach assertion through "scriptures exemplifying assertiveness." Psychology professor Edward W. C. McAllister (1975), advocates assertiveness training for Christian therapists because many of their religious clients view nonassertiveness as *part* of their Christianity.

Two books which discuss assertiveness and religion are David Augsburger's *Anger and Assertiveness in Pastoral Care* (1979), and Michael Emmons and David Richardson's *The Assertive Christian* (1981). Augsburger illustrates how pastors can handle anger and aggression in constructive ways. Emmons and Richardson consider such religious-assertive issues as meekness, anger, guilt, the assertiveness of Jesus. (Incidentally, we are aware of no work relating assertiveness to religions other than Christian.)

Nurses and Allied Medical Personnel. Health care delivery systems have long been controlled as benevolent dictatorships by physicians. Recently, however, nurses and other health care professionals have assumed more important roles in delivery of services to patients. As both cause and result, these health care staff are developing greater independence and personal/professional assertiveness. Nurse Practitioners, for example, proceed independently under only limited physician supervision. Many services are now administered by Physician's Assistants. Assertiveness training has become a vital part of nursing education programs throughout the country (Herman, 1977, 1978; Faily, Hensley, Rich, 1979). And many health care professionals are advocating greater *patient* assertiveness as well! In a very important and therapeutic way, health care delivery is becoming a cooperative venture, involving physician, staff, and patient, and AT is a valuable tool in that process. (Keet and Nelson, 1986)

Rehabilitation Counselors. A particularly exciting area of AT application has evolved in work with handicapped and retarded persons. Although results are highly variable, and the work very difficult, a number of professionals have reported success in training for employment interviews, obtaining medical, educational and social services, dealing with relatives who treat the handicapped adult "like a child," gaining enough confidence to enroll in college, and developing skills in general social interaction. Issue 13 of the now defunct *ASSERT* newsletter described several such programs.

Management and Human Resources Development. Individuals who are concerned with staff development in industrial and/or governmental organizations may find that a systematic effort to train management and sales personnel in assertiveness will pay big dividends. Group training methods will be useful in large organizations, and assertiveness training can be effectively incorporated into other management development or staff training programs.

Supervisorial personnel who understand, and can apply the assertive (nonaggressive) model to their interactions with subordinates are too few, and more effective management teams can be developed utilizing AT as a key to recognition of the rights and organizational parameters of each employee. For example, a supervisor who can firmly reprimand a subordinate's *error* without devastating that *person* is a valuable asset in any organization. Also, of course, the lower-level employee who can honestly and constructively criticize supervisors or the operation — in an assertive fashion — without fear on the one hand, or aggressive attack on the other, can be a significant contributor to organizational productivity, and a happier worker (Shaw, 1979).

Among the many books which have dealt effectively with this topic are the second edition of Stanlee Phelps and Nancy Austin's *The Assertive Woman* (1987), Tom Peters and Nancy Austin's *A Passion for Excellence* (1985), Susanne Drury's *Assertive Supervision* (1984), and Linda MacNeilage and Kathleen Adams' *Assertiveness at Work* (1982).

Leadership Training for Community Organizations. Effective leadership at all levels is perhaps the greatest single area of difficulty facing volunteer community groups. School-parent associations, service clubs, auxiliaries, women's clubs, interest groups, churches, youth activities, social clubs, even community action agencies and political parties suffer from a lack of persons willing and able to assume key responsibilities. While it is obvious that lack of time for such involvement is an important reason for the dearth of willing individuals, it is also true that many persons simply consider themselves inadequately prepared to accept responsibility for a committee, or a club, or a community activity (Lawson, et al., 1982). Leadership development in such groups — from securing volunteers for an arrangements committee to convincing candidates to accept the nominating committee's call to the presidency or chairmanship — can be enhanced by including a program of assertive behavior development for the "rank and file" membership as well as for those who have already attained identified leadership roles.

On a larger scale, groups which would "change the world" are finding assertive action, which reponds to the needs of those in opposition to their goals, can often make greater progress than confrontations and disruptions. Psychology professor Neil Wollman and his colleagues have produced a volume of ideas on application of psychological principles to the peace movement which includes assertive approaches among its many suggestions (Wollman, 1985).

Youth Workers. Adult leaders in such organizations as YM and YWCA's, YM and YWHA's, Boy and Girl Scouts, 4-H, Future Farmers, community recreation programs, church and church school youth groups, and summer camps have considerable opportunity to observe the behavior of young people, notably in social settings where the youngsters are working and/or playing with their fellows. The apathetic, disinterested or asocial youth who is observed in such a group may well be nonassertive, may fear failure and subsequent rejection, refuse to try anything, or attempt to dominate peers by being brash and abrasive. The sensitive adult who notes such behavior may be able to help this young person by providing a non-threatening, secure environment (perhaps on a one-to-one basis at first) in which the youth can feel safe in trying some new activity. The process of shaping more confident behavior may be slow, but it can provide the youngster with opportunities to make choices among alternative ways of acting. This step toward independence is an important quality of all such youth-oriented programs.

Journalism. A university journalism instructor noticed the potential use of AT with photography students and asked us to make presentations and give demonstrations in his classes. We have found that assertive concepts can be important in the improvement of photographic skills. If a photographer is either overly shy and cautious or too overbearing and pushy, the results will be affected. Being assertive rather than aggressive may help one to minimize the physical abuse and even lawsuits that press photographers too often experience.

Another application for journalists is in development of interviewing skills. For instance, how do you assertively approach the subject and obtain the story you need? How do you handle a domineering person who wants to take over the interview? What should you say if you deeply disagree with the person's views? Is there a way to put at ease a subject who is anxious or is trying too hard? Or to confront the person who feeds you information which you already know is false? All of these situations are natural opportunities for the assertive processes.

Human Liberation. Many women have learned not to feel good about themselves and their abilities for a variety of reasons. Everyone has a perfect right to feel good about themselves and to be able assertively to stand up for themselves in life. Most of us are familiar with aggressive behavior in the service of a "cause." And we are equally put off by the nonassertive counterpart, the frail effort which displays little spunk and independence.

There now exist many broadly-based community programs of treatment for persons typically denied access to therapeutic services: the poor, minorities, working people. Women's consciousness efforts have had remarkable effects in large and small communities throughout the world.

Application of assertive behavior principles is useful to any oppressed group; ethnic minorities, students, children, laborers, the poor, the aged, gays, the disabled... the list goes on. All have much to gain from assertion of their rights in accordance with the fundamental processes described in *Your Perfect Right*.

The Center for Third World Organizing, of Oakland, California, (1984) has prepared a guide for increasing one's effectiveness in dealing with the social institutions which control access to aid programs. *Surviving America* describes the rights of U.S. citizens in such areas as social security, veteran's assistance, Aid to Families with Dependent Children, tenant's rights, food stamps, Medicaid/Medicare, employment, education, civil rights and the courts. Each of these programs is more accessible to the *assertive* client. Trainers must be aware of the availability of such resources if they are to be of greatest benefit to those they hope to serve.

Others. AT with juvenile delinquents, consumers, the disabled, divorced persons, alcohol and substance abusers, senior citizens, families, and in weight control programs are among the myriad applications of which we are aware.

The examples given in this chapter are by no means all-inclusive. The reader is encouraged to consult the literature, colleagues and friends, and to reflect on his/her own experience for other relevant applications of assertiveness training.

It should be noted, however, that although AT may have been utilized with a particular population — even successfully — there are no assurances that it will be of benefit to any individual or group. Facilitators are urged to thoroughly *assess* the needs of their clients — including those in "public" workshops — to determine the appropriateness of their interventions.

We urge professionals to integrate AT into a comprehensive approach to total client needs, and to operate within principles which advocate responsible self-expression which is non-hurtful to others.

29

SYNTHESIS

There are many ways to grow.

Social skills/assertiveness training is a complex process comprised of many elements. Goal clarification, skill training, cognitive restructuring, anxiety reduction, emotional expression, and the wide variety of techniques possible to achieve each, weave an intricate web of change mechanisms.

How is the trainer to decide? Surely there is not time in anyone's schedule to include all the possibilities!

AT/SST is something of a paradox. While on the surface it appears among the simplest of behavior change procedures, an in-depth examination makes clear that it must be thoughtfully adapted to the needs of each individual client (or at the least to each client group). Such individualization requires careful assessment, precise selection of procedures, and skilled practice of those techniques which are selected.

A few guides for synthesis:

• Don't attempt to conduct training until you are adequately prepared (see Chapter 21 and the *Principles for Ethical Practice of Assertive Behavior Training*).

• Assess trainee needs in terms of behavioral skills, attitudes toward self and toward assertiveness, anxiety and other obstacles to effective self-expression.

• Develop professional skills with at least one proven approach in each area. Select carefully from among the many approaches, then learn well those you choose.

• Apply your skills with care, continuously monitoring client progress, and putting emphasis where need is greatest. Avoid "canned" training — the same thing does not work for everyone.

• Keep your practice up to date by regular examination of the literature. It is amazing how fast new procedures are found valuable, and old ones go out of date.

• Keep yourself up to date by monitoring and evaluating your work. Use audio and videotape, peer review, supervision, client feedback — all the methods you use with your trainees — to keep your own techniques sharp.

Cognitive therapies, behavior therapies, and humanistic therapies all have contributed much to the development and practice of assertiveness training. Indeed, AT may be the only procedure where all three may be found as "comfortable bedfellows."

No one has a corner on truth, but those of us whose principal interest is *application* of knowledge may feel confident that "enlightened eclecticism" is still the honorable path.

• Yes, trainees do need to deal with their thoughts, attitudes, and self-statements, as the cognitive people have been telling us.

• And yes, overt behavioral skills are the most evident and "trainable" dimension of self expression. The behavior therapists are clearly right in that regard.

• Behavioral skills and cognitions notwithstanding, clients who lack awareness of their feelings and goals will find little to be assertive about, as we have been taught by humanistic psychology.

Each theory/methodology contains some truth. And it is to each that responsible therapists turn for help, *depending upon the needs of the individual client.*

Prepare yourself carefully.

Assess your trainees with equal care.

And practice AT ethically and responsibly.

PRINCIPLES FOR ETHICAL PRACTICE
OF ASSERTIVE BEHAVIOR TRAINING

As AT gained in popularity during the mid-1970's, an increasing concern developed among responsible practitioners for the misuse of the process: unqualified trainers, illegitimate purposes, contraindicated clients. At the December 1975 meeting of the Association for Advancement of Behavior Therapy in San Francisco, a group of nationally recognized AT professionals met to initiate work on a statement of ethical principles. The following statement is the result of their work.

Further discussion of this proposal occurred at the First International Conference on Assertive Behavior Training in Washington, D.C., in August, 1976, and at the Association for Advancement of Behavior Therapy in New York City, December, 1976. Although no amendments to the original statement have been formalized, considerable concern has been expressed about the academic credentials suggested herein for qualifying facilitators. It is likely that a competency based criterion for qualification will emerge.

Moreover, AABT itself is preparing a statement of ethics for the practice of behavior therapy generally, which may have direct application to AT, although AT is not considered solely a "behavior therapy" by a considerable number of its practitioners.

Meanwhile, however, this statement remains the only public declaration by a group of professionals which is directed toward greater ethical responsibility in the practice of AT. Practitioners are urged to consider its implications for their own work.

With the increasing popularity of assertive behavior training, a quality of "faddishness" has become evident, and there are frequent reports of ethically irresponsible practices (and practitioners). We hear of trainers who, for example, do not adequately differentiate assertion and aggression. Others have failed to advocate proper ethical responsibility and caution to clients—e.g., failed to alert them to and/or prepare them for the possibility of retaliation or other highly negative reactions from others.

The following statement of "Principles for Ethical Practice of Assertive Behavior Training" is the work of the professional psychologists and educators listed below, who are actively engaged in the practice of facilitating assertive behavior (also referred to as "assertive therapy," "social skills training," "personal effectiveness training," and "AT"). We don't intend by this statement to discourage untrained individuals from becoming more assertive on their own, and we don't advocate that one must have extensive credentials in order to be of help to friends and relatives. Rather, these principles are offered to help foster responsible and ethical teaching and practice by human services professionals. Others who wish to enhance their own assertiveness or that of associates are encouraged to do so, with awareness of their own limitations, and of the importance of seeking help from a qualified therapist/trainer when necessary.

We hereby declare support for and adherence to the statement of principles, and invite responsible professionals in our own and other fields who use these techniques to join us in advocating and practicing these principles.

Robert E. Alberti, Ph.D.
Michael L. Emmons, Ph.D.
San Luis Obispo, CA

Lynne Garnett, Ph.D.
Counseling Psychologist
Seattle, WA

Iris G. Fodor, Ph.D.
Associate Professor, Educational Psychology
New York University, Washington Square
New York, NY

Patricia Jakubowski, Ed.D.
Associate Professor, Behavioral Studies
University of Missouri
St. Louis, MO

John Galassi, Ph.D.
School of Education
University of North Carolina
Chapel Hill, NC

Janet L. Wolfe, Ph.D.
Director of Clinical Services
Institute for Advanced Study in Rational
  Psychotherapy
New York, NY

Merna D. Galassi, Ed.D.
Meredith College
Raleigh, NC

1. Definition of Assertive Behavior

For purposes of these principles and the ethical framework expressed herein, we define assertive behavior as that complex of behaviors, emitted by a person in an interpersonal context, which express that person's feelings, attitudes, wishes, opinions or rights directly, firmly, and honestly, while respecting the feelings, attitudes, wishes, opinions and rights of the other person(s). Such behavior may include the expression of such emotions as anger, fear, caring, hope, joy, despair, indignance, embarrassment, but in any event is expressed in a manner which does not violate the rights of others. Assertive behavior is differentiated from aggressive behavior which, while expressive of one person's feelings, attitudes, wishes, opinions or rights, does not respect those characteristics in others.

While this definition is intended to be comprehensive, it is recognized that any adequate definition of assertive behavior must consider several dimensions:

A. *Intent:* behavior classified as assertive is not intended by its author to be hurtful of others.

B. *Behavior:* behavior classified as assertive would be evaluated by an "objective observer" as itself honest, direct, expressive and non-destructive of others.

C. *Effects:* behavior classified as assertive has the effect upon the receiver of a direct and non-destructive message, by which a "reasonable person" would not be hurt.

D. *Socio-cultural Context:* behavior classified as assertive is appropriate to the environment and culture in which it is exhibited, and may not be considered "assertive" in a different socio-cultural environment.

2. Client Self-Determination

These principles recognize and affirm the inherent dignity and the equal and inalienable rights of all members of the human family, as proclaimed in the "Universal Declaration of Human Rights" endorsed by the General Assembly of the United Nations.

Pursuant to the precepts of the Declaration, each client (trainee, patient) who seeks assertive behavior training shall be treated as a person of value, with all of the freedoms and rights expressed in the Declaration. No procedure shall be utilized in the name of assertive behavior training which would violate those freedoms or rights.

Informed client self-determination shall guide all such interventions:

A. the client shall be fully informed in advance of all procedures to be utilized;
B. the client shall have the freedom to choose to participate or not at any point in the intervention;
C. the client who is institutionalized shall be similarly treated with respect and without coercion, insofar as is possible within the institutional environment.
D. the client shall be provided with explicit definitions of assertiveness and assertive training.
E. the client shall be fully informed as to the education, training, experience or other qualifications of the assertive trainer(s).
F. the client shall be informed as to the goals and potential outcomes of assertive training, including potentially high levels of anxiety, and possible negative reactions from others.
G. the client shall be fully informed as to the responsibility of the assertion trainer(s) and the client(s).
H. the client shall be informed as to the ethics and employment of confidentiality guidelines as they pertain to various assertive training settings (e.g. clinical vs. non-clinical).

3. Qualifications of Facilitators

Assertive behavior training is essentially a therapeutic procedure, although frequently practiced in a variety of settings by professionals not otherwise engaged in rendering a ''psychological'' service. Persons in any professional role who engage in helping others to change their behavior, attitudes, and interpersonal relationships must understand human behavior at a level commensurate with the level of their interventions.

3.1 General Qualifications

We support the following minimum, general qualifications for facilitators at all levels of intervention (including ''trainers in training''—preservice or inservice—who are preparing for professional service in a recognized human services field, and who may be conducting assertive behavior training under supervision as part of a research project or practicum):

A. Fundamental understanding of the principles of learning and behavior (equivalent to completion of a rigorous undergraduate level course in learning theory);
B. Fundamental understanding of anxiety and its effects upon behavior (equivalent to completion of a rigorous undergraduate level course in abnormal psychology);
C. Knowledge of the limitations, contraindications and potential dangers of assertive behavior training; familiarity with theory and research in the area.
D. Satisfactory evidence of competent performance as a facilitator, as observed by a qualified trainer, is strongly recommended for all professionals, particularly for those who do not possess a doctorate or an equivalent level of training. Such evidence would most ideally be supported by:
   1) participation in at least ten (10) hours of assertive behavior training as a client (trainee, patient); and
   2) participation in at least ten (10) hours of assertive behavior training as a facilitator under supervision.

3.2 Specific Qualifications

The following additional qualifications are considered to be the minimum expected for facilitators at the indicated levels of intervention:

A. *Assertive behavior training*, including non-clinical workshops, groups, and individual client training aimed at teaching assertive skills to those persons who require only encouragement and specific skill training, and in whom no serious emotional deficiency or pathology is evident.

1) For trainers in programs conducted under the sponsorship of a recognized human services agency, school, governmental or corporate entity, church, or community organization:
   a) An advanced degree in a recognized field of human services (e.g. psychology, counseling, social work, medicine, public health, nursing, education, human development, theology/divinity), including at least one term of field experience in a human services agency supervised by a qualified trainer; *or*
   b) certification as a minister, public school teacher, social worker, physician, counselor, nurse, or clinical, counseling, educational, or school psychologist, or similar human services professional, as recognized by the state wherein employed or by the recognized state or national professional society in the indicated discipline; *or*
   c) one year of paid counseling experience in a recognized human services agency, supervised by a qualified trainer; *or*
   d) qualification under items 3.2B or 3.2C below.

2) For trainers in programs including interventions at the level defined in this item (3.2A), but without agency/organization sponsorship:
   a) An advanced degree in a recognized field of human services (e.g. psychology, counseling, social work, medicine, public health, nursing, education, human development, theology/divinity) including at least one term of field experience in a human services agency supervised by a qualified trainer; *and*
   b) certification as a minister, social worker, physician, counselor, nurse, or clinical, counseling, educational, or school psychologist, or similar human services professional, as recognized by the state wherein employed or by the recognized state or national professional society in the indicated discipline; *or*
   c) qualification under items 3.2B or 3.2C below.

B. *Assertive behavior therapy*, including clinical interventions designed to assist persons who are severely inhibited by anxiety, or who are significantly deficient in social skills, or who are controlled by aggression, or who evidence pathology, or for whom other therapeutic procedures are indicated:
1) For therapists in programs conducted under the sponsorship of a recognized human services agency, school, governmental or corporate entity, church, or community organization:
   a) An advanced degree in a recognized field of human services (e.g. psychology, counseling, social work, medicine, public health, nursing, education, human development, theology/divinity) including at least one term of field experience in a human services agency supervised by a qualified trainer; *or*
   b) certification as a minister, social worker, physician, counselor, nurse, or clinical, counseling, educational, or school psychologist, as recognized by the state wherein employed or by the recognized state or national professional society in the indicated discipline; *or*
   c) qualification under item 3.2C below.

2) For therapists employing interventions at the level defined in this item (3.2B), but without agency/organization sponsorship:
   a) An advanced degree in a recognized field of human services (e.g. psychology,

counseling, social work, medicine, public health, nursing, education, human development, theology/divinity) including at least one term of field experience in a human services agency supervised by a qualified trainer; *and*

b) certification as minister, social worker, physician, counselor, nurse, or clinical, counseling, educational, or school psychologist, as recognized by the state wherein employed or by the recognized state or national professional society in the indicated discipline; *and*

c) at least one year of paid professional experience in a recognized human services agency, supervised by a qualified trainer; *or*

d) qualification under item 3.2C below.

C. *Training of trainers*, including preparation of other professionals to offer assertive behavior training/therapy to clients, in school, agency, organization, or individual settings.

1) A doctoral degree in a recognized field of human services (e.g. psychology, counseling, social work, medicine, public health, nursing, education, human development, theology/divinity) including at least one term of field experience in a human services agency supervised by a qualified trainer; *and*

2) certification as a minister, social worker, physician, counselor, nurse, or clinical, counseling, educational, or school psychologist, as recognized by the state wherein employed, or by the recognized state or national professional society in the indicated discipline; *and*

3) at least one year of paid professional experience in a recognized human services agency, supervised by a qualified trainer; *and*

4) advanced study in assertive behavior training/therapy, including at least two of the following:

a) At least thirty (30) hours of facilitation with clients;

b) participation in at least two different workshops at professional meetings or professional training institutes:

c) contribution to the professional literature in the field.

3.3 We recognize that counselors and psychologists are not certified by each state. In states wherein no such certification is provided, unless contrary to local statute, we acknowledge the legitimacy of professionals who: A) are otherwise qualified under the provisions of items 3.1 and 3.2; and B) would be eligible for certification as a counselor or psychologist in another state.

3.4 We do not consider that participation in one or two workshops on assertive behavior, even though conducted by a professional with an advanced degree, is adequate qualification to offer assertive behavior training to others, *unless the additional qualifications* of items 3.1 and 3.2 are also met.

3.5 These qualifications are presented as *standards* for professional facilitators of assertive behavior. No ''certification'' or ''qualifying'' agency is hereby proposed. Rather, it is incumbent upon each professional to evaluate himself/herself as a trainer/therapist according to these standards, and to make explicit to clients the adequacy of his/her qualifications as a facilitator.

4. Ethical Behavior of Facilitators

Since the encouragement and facilitation of assertive behavior is essentially a *therapeutic* procedure, the ethical standards most applicable to the practice of assertive behavior training are those of psychologists. We recognize that many persons who practice some form of assertive behavior training are not otherwise engaged in rendering a "psychological" service (i.e. teachers, personnel/training directors). To all we support the statement of "Ethical Standards for Psychologists" as adopted by the American Psychological Association as the standard of ethical behavior by which assertive behavior training shall be conducted.

We recognize that the methodology employed in assertive behavior training may include a wide range of procedures, some of which are of unproven value. It is the responsibility of the facilitators to inform clients of any experimental procedures. Under no circumstances should the facilitator "guarantee" a specific outcome from an intervention.

5. Appropriateness of Assertive Behavior Training Interventions

Assertive behavior training, as any intervention oriented toward helping people change, may be applied under a wide range of conditions, yet its appropriateness must be evaluated in each individual case. The responsible selection of assertive behavior training for a particular intervention must include attention to at least the following dimensions:

A. *Client:* The personal characteristics of the client in question (age, sex, ethnicity, institutionalization, capacity for informed choice, physical and psychological functionality).

B. *Problem/Goals:* The purpose for which professional help has been sought or recommended (job skills, severe inhibition, anxiety reduction, overcome aggression).

C. *Facilitator:* The personal and professional qualifications of the facilitator in question (age, sex, ethnicity, skills, understanding, ethics—see also Principles 3 and 4 above).

D. *Setting:* The characteristics of the setting in which the intervention is conducted (home, school, business, agency, clinic, hospital, prison). Is the client free to choose? Is the facilitator's effectiveness systematically evaluated?

E. *Time/Duration:* The duration of the intervention. Does the time involved represent a brief word of encouragement, a formal training workshop, an intensive and long-term therapeutic effort?

F. *Method:* The nature of the intervention. Is it "packaged" procedure or tailored to client needs? Is training based on sound principles of learning and behavior? Is there clear differentiation of aggressiveness, assertiveness and other concepts? Are definitions, techniques, procedures and purposes clarified? Is care taken to encourage small, successful steps and to minimize punishing consequences? Are any suggested "homework assignments" presented with adequate supervision, responsibility, and sensitivity to the effect upon significant others of the client's behavior change efforts? Are clients informed that assertiveness "doesn't always work?"

G. *Outcome:* Are there follow-up procedures, either by self-report or other post-test procedures?

6. Social Responsibility

Assertive behavior training shall be conducted within the law. Trainers and clients are encouraged to work assertively to change those laws which they consider need to be changed, and to modify the social system in ways they believe appropriate—in particular to extend the boundaries of human rights. Toward these ends, trainers are encouraged to facilitate responsible change skills via assertive behavior training. All those who practice, teach, or do research on assertive behavior are urged to advocate caution and ethical responsibility in application of the technique, in accordance with these Principles.

REFERENCES AND BIBLIOGRAPHY

Alberti, R. (Ed). (1977). *Assertiveness: Innovations, Applications, Issues.* San Luis Obispo, California: Impact Publishers, Inc. (Now out of print, but available in many libraries.)

Alberti, R.E. (1976). Was that *assertive* or *aggressive? ASSERT: The Newsletter of Assertive Behavior, 1* (7), 2.

Alberti, R.E. & Emmons, M.L. (1976). Assertion training in marital counseling, *Journal of Marriage and Family Counseling,* 49-54.

Alberti, R.E. & Emmons, M.L. *Your Perfect Right: A Guide to Assertive Behavior.* San Luis Obispo, California: Impact Publishers, Inc., 1970 (lst edition), 1974 (2nd edition), 1978 (3rd edition), 1982 (4th edition), 1986 (5th edition), 1990 (6th edition).

Alden, L. & Cappe, R. (1981). Nonassertiveness: Skill deficit or selective self-evaluation? *Behavior Therapy, 12,* 107-115.

Allen, E.J., Jr. (1976). Repression-sensitization and the effect of assertion on anxiety. Senior Research Paper. St. Meinrad College, St. Meinrad, Indiana.

Alschuler, C.F. & Alschuler, A.S. (1984). Developing healthy responses to anger: The counselor's role. *Journal of Counseling and Development, 63,* 26-29.

Andrasik, F, Heimberg, R.G., Edlund, S.R. & Blankenberg, R. (1981). Assessing the reliability levels of self-report assertion inventories. *Journal of Consulting and Clinical Psychology, 49,* 142-144.

Ardrey, R. (1966). *The Territorial Imperative.* New York: Atheneum.

Argyle, M., Alkema, F., & Gilmour, R. (1972). The communication of friendly and hostile attitudes by verbal and non-verbal signals. *European Journal of Social Psychology, I,* 385-402.

Arrick, M.C., Voss, J.R. & Rimm, D.C. (1981). The relative efficacy of thought-stopping and covert assertion. *Behaviour Research and Therapy, 19,* 17-24.

Augsberger, D. (1979). *Anger and Assertiveness in Pastoral Care.* Philadelphia: Fortress Press.

Averill, J. (1981). Studies on anger and aggression. Paper presented at the American Psychological Association Convention, Los Angeles.

Averill, J. (1982). *Anger and Aggression.* New York: Springer-Verlag, 1982.

Bach, G. & Wyden, P. (1968). *Creative Aggression.* New York: William Morrow and Company, Inc.

Baer, J. (1976). *How to Be an Assertive* (not Aggressive) *Woman in Life, in Love, and on the Job.* New York: Signet (New American Library).

Bandura, A. (1973). *Aggression: A Social Learning Analysis.* Englewood Cliffs, New Jersey: Prentice-Hall.

Bandura, A. (1969). *Principles of Behavior Modification.* New York: Holt, Rinehart, Winston.

Bates, H.D. & Zimmerman, S.F. (1971). Toward the development of a screening scale for assertive training. *Psychological Reports, 28,* 99-107.

Bates, P. (1980). The effectiveness of interpersonal skills training on the social skill acquisition of moderately and mildly retarded adults. *Journal of applied behavior Analysis, 13,* 237-248.

Beck, A. (1986). Cognitive therapy: A sign of retrogression or progress? *The Behavior Therapist, 9* (1), 2-3.

Beck, A.T. (1976). *Cognitive Therapy and the Emotional disorders.* New York: International Universities Press.

Beck, A.T., Rush, A.J., Shaw, B.F., & Emery, G. (1979). *Cognitive Therapy of Depression.* New York: Guilford Press.

Beck, J.G. & Heimberg, R.G. (1983). Self-report assessment of assertive behavior: A critical analysis. *Behavior Modification, 7,* 451-487.

Bedrosian, R.C., & Beck, A.T. (1980). Principles of cognitive therapy. In M. J. Mahoney (Ed.), *Psychotherapy Process: Current Issues and Future Directions.* New York: Plenum.

Bellack, A.S., & Hersen, M. (1977). *Behavior Modification: An Introductory Text.* Baltimore: Williams & Wilkins.

Bellack, A., & Hersen, M. (Eds.) (1979). *Research and Practice in Social Skills Training.* New York: Plenum Press.

Berah, E.F. (1981). Influence of scheduling variations on the effectiveness of a group assertion training program for women. *Journal of Counseling Psychology, 28* (3), 265-268.

Berkowitz, L. (1965). The concept of aggressive drive: some additional considerations. In L. Berkowitz (Ed.), *Advances in Experimental Social Psychology,* Vol. 2. New York: Academic Press.

Berkowitz, L. (1969). *Roots of Aggression: A Re-Examination of the Frustration-Aggression Hypothesis.* New York: Atherton Press.

Berkowitz, L. (1978). What ever happened to the frustration-aggression hypothesis? *American Behavioral Scientist, 21,* 691-708.

Bernard, J.M. (1980). Assertiveness in children. *Psychological Reports, 46,* 935-938.

Berrier, G.D., Galassi, J.P. & Mullinix, S.D. (1981). A comparison of matched clinical and analogue subjects on variables pertinent to the treatment of assertion deficits. *Journal of Consulting and Clinical Psychology, 49,* 980-981.

Biaggio, M.K. (1980). Assessment of anger arousal. *Journal of Personality Assessment, 44,* 289-298.

Blau, J.S. (1980). Changes in assertiveness and marital satisfaction after participation in an assertiveness training group. *Behavioral Group Therapy,* 68-83.

Bodner, G. (1975). The role of assessment in assertion training. *The Counseling Psychologist, 5,* 90-96.

Bohart, A.C. (1980). Toward a cognitive theory of catharsis. *Psychotherapy: Theory, Research and Practice,* 17, 192-201.

Bolles, R.N. (1990). *What Color Is Your Parachute?* Berkeley, CA: Ten Speed Press (annual).

Bolsinger, S. & McMinn, M. (1989, Oct.) Assertiveness training and Christian values. *Counseling and Values,* 34:21-31.

Bordewick, M.C. & Bornstein, P.H. (1980). Examination of multiple cognitive response dimensions among differentially assertive individuals. *Behavior Therapy, 11,* 440-448.

Borkovec, T.D., Weerts, T.C. & Bernstein, D.A. (1977) Assessment of anxiety. In A.R. Ciminero, K.S. Calhoun & H. Adams (Eds.), *Handbook of Behavioral Assessment.* New York: Wiley, 1977.

Bower, S.A. & Bower, G.H. (1976). *Asserting Yourself.* Reading: MA: Addison-Wesley.

Brooks, G.R. & Richardson, F.C. (1980). Emotional skills training: A treatment program for duodenal ulcer. *Behavior Therapy, 11,* 198-207.

Brown, S.D. & Brown, L.W. (1980). Trends in assertion training research and practice: A content analysis of the published literature. *Journal of Clinical Psychology, 36,* 265-269.

Bruch, M.A. (1981). A task analysis of assertive behavior revisited: Replication and extension. *Behavior Therapy, 12,* 217-230.

Bruch, M.A., Haase, R.F., & Purcell, M.J. (1984). Content dimensions of self-statements in assertive situations: A factor analysis of two measures. *Cognitive Therapy and Research, 8* (2), 173-186.

Bruch, M.A., Heisler, B.D. & Conroy, C.G. (1981). Effects of conceptual complexity on assertive behavior. *Journal of Counseling Psychology, 28,* 377-385.

Buell, G. & Snyder, J. (1981). Assertiveness training with children. *Psychological Reports, 49,* 71-80.

Cacioppo, J. & Petty, R. (1981). Inductive techniques for cognitive assessment: The thought listing procedure. In T. Merluzzi, C. Glass, & M. Genest (Eds.), *Cognitive Assessment.* New York: Guilford.

Cameron, D.E. (1951). The conversion of passivity into normal self-assertion. *American Journal of Psychiatry, 108,* 98.

Camplese, D.A. & Camplese, K.F. (1982). Assertive time out procedure: A systematic approach to classroom discipline. *Reading Improvement, 19,* 292-295.

Canter, L. (1988, Jan.) Assertive discipline and the search for the perfect classroom. *Young Children,* 43 (2): 24ff.

Canter, L. (1988, Oct.) Let the educator beware. *Educational Leadership,* 46 (2): 71-73.

Canter, L. (1989, Sept.) Assertive discipline — more than names on the board and beans in a jar. *Phi Delta Kappan,* 57-61.

Canter, L. & Canter, M. (1976). *Assertive Discipline. Los Angeles: Canter and Associates.*

Carducci, D., J. (1980). Positive peer culture and assertiveness training: Complementary modalities for dealing with disturbed and disturbing adolescents in the classroom. *Behavioral Disorders, 5,* 156-162.

Cash, T.F. (1984). The irrational beliefs test: Its relationship with cognitive-behavioral traits and depression. *Journal of Clinical Psychology, 40,* 1399-1405.

Cautela, J., Flannery, R. & Hanley, E. (1974). Covert modeling: An experimental test. *Behavior Therapy, 5,,* 494-502.

Center for Third World Organizing (1984). *Surviving America.* Oakland, California: Author (3861 Martin Luther King Jr. Way, 94609).

Chambless, D.L., Hunter, K. & Jackson, A. (1982). Social anxiety and assertiveness: A comparison of the correlations in phobic and college student samples. *Behavior Research and Therapy, 20,* 403-404.

Cheek, D.K. (1976). *Assertive Black...Puzzled White.* Atascadero, California: Author (P.O. Box 1476, 93422).

Chittenden, G.E. (1942). An experimental study in measuring and modifying assertive behavior in young children. *Monographs of the Society for Research in Child Development, 7* (1, Serial #31).

Cianni-Surridge, M. & Horan, J. (1983). On the wisdom of assertive job-seeking behavior. *Journal of Counseling Psychology, 30,* 209-214.

Connelly, D. (1988, Sept.) Increasing the intensity of play of nonassertive athletes. *Sport Psychologist, 2* (3): 255-265.

Cooley, M.L. & Hollandsworth, J.G., Jr. (1977). A strategy for teaching verbal content of assertive responses. In R.E. Alberti (Ed.), *Assertiveness: Innovations, Applications, Issues.* San Luis Obispo, California: Impact Publishers, Inc.

Corey, G. & Corey, M. (1982). *Groups: Process and Practice* (Second Edition). Monterey, California: Brooks-Cole.

Cotler, S.B. & Cotler, S.M. (1977). Four myths of nonassertiveness in the work environment. In R.E. Alberti (Ed.), *Assertiveness: Innovations, Applications, Issues.* San Luis Obispo, California: Impact Publishers, Inc., 1977.

Cotler, S.B. & Guerra, J.J. (1976). *Assertion Training: A Humanistic-Behavioral Guide to Self-Dignity.* Champaign: Research Press.

Cottraux, J., Bollard, E., Defayolle, M. (1982). Behavioral and bodily self-concept changes after assertive training: A pilot study. *Acta Psychiatrica Belgica, 82,* 136-146.

Crassini, B., Law, H.G. & Wilson, E. (1979). Sex differences in assertive behavior? *Australian Journal of Psychology, 31* (1), 15-19.

Crockenberg, V. (1982). Assertive discipline: A dissent. *California Journal of Teacher Education, 9,* 59-74.

Cummins, D.E. (1978). On the use of unobtrusive measures of assertion. *ASSERT: The Newsletter of Assertive Behavior and Personal Development,* February, p. 1.

Curran, J.P., et al. (1980). Social skill and social anxiety: Self-report measurement in a psychiatric population. *Behavior Modification, 4* (4), 493-512.

Curwin, R., & Mendler, M. (1988, Oct.). Packaged discipline programs: let the buyer beware. *Educational Leadership, 46* (2): 68-71.

Curwin, R., et al. (1989, Mar.). We repeat: let the buyer beware. A response to Canter. *Educational Leadership, 46* (6): 83.

Dalali, I.D. (1971). The effect of active-assertion and feeling clarification training on factor analyzed measures of assertion. Doctoral dissertation, University of California, Los Angeles. *Dissertation Abstracts International, 32,* 1B-1291B, University Microfilms No. 71-21, 322.

D'Amico, W. (1976). *Revised Rathus Assertiveness Scale for Children, Grades 3-8.* Marblehead, Mass.: Educational Counseling and Consulting Services.

Delehanty, R. (1982). Changes in assertiveness and changes in orgasmic response occurring with sexual therapy for pre-orgasmic women. *Journal of Sex and Marital Therapy, 8,* 198-208.

Deluty, R.H. (1981). Alternative-thinking ability of aggressive, assertive and submissive children. *Cognitive Therapy and Research, 5,* 309-312.

Dodson, K. (1988). *Handbook of Cognitive-Behavioral Therapies.* New York: Guilford Press.

Dowrick, P.W. & Gilligan, C.A. (1985). Social skills and children: An annotated bibliography. *The Behavior Therapist, 8* (10), 211-213.

Doyle, M.A. & Biaggio, M.K. (1981). Expression of anger as a function of assertiveness and sex. *Journal of Clinical Psychology, 37,* 154-157.

Drury, S. (1984), *Assertive Supervision.* Champaign, IL: Research Press.

Eastridge, M.D. (1984). A comparison of flooding, cognitive behavior modification, and assertiveness training as anger control treatments for women. *Dissertation Abstracts International, 44(12-B),* 3929.

Eisler, R.M., Miller, P.M., & Hersen, M. (1973). Components of assertive behavior. *Journal of Clinical Psychology, 29,* 295-299.

Eisler, R.M., Hersen, M., & Miller, P.M. (1973). Effects of modeling components of assertive behavior. *Journal of Behavior Therapy and Experimental Psychiatry, 4,* 1-6.

Eisler, R.M., Hersen, M., Miller, P.M., & Blanchard, E.B. (1975). Situational determinants of assertive behaviors. *Journal of Consulting and Clinical Psychology, 43,* 330-341.

Eisler, R., Fredericksen, L., & Peterson, G. (1978), the relationship of cognitive variables to the expression of assertiveness. *Behavior Therapy,* 9:419-427.

Elder, J.P., Edelstein, B.A. & Fremouw, W.J. (1981). Client by treatment interactions in response acquisition and cognitive restructuring approaches. *Cognitive Therapy & Research, 5* (2), 203-210.

Elgin, S.H. (1987). *The Last Word on the Gentle Art of Verbal Self-Defense.* New York: Prentice-Hall.

Ellis, A. (1980). Rational Emotive Therapy and Cognitive Behavior Therapy: Similarities and differences. *Cognitive Therapy and Research, 4* (4), 325-340.

Ellis, A. & Harper, R. (1979). *A New Guide to Rational Living.* Englewood Cliffs, New Jersey: Prentice-Hall; Hollywood: Wilshire-Brooks/Cole.

Emery, G. (1984). *Own Your Own Life.* New York: Signet.

Emery, G., Hollon, S.D. & Bedrosian, R.C. (Eds.). (1981). *New Directions in Cognitive Therapy.* New York, London: Guilford Press.

Emmelkamp, P.M., Van der Hout, A. & de Vries, K. (1983). Assertive training for agoraphobics. *Behaviour Research and Therapy, 21,* 63-68.

Emmelkamp, P.M. (1980). Agoraphobics' interpersonal problems: Their role in the effects of exposure *in vivo* therapy. *Archives of General Psychiatry, 37,* 1303-1306.

Emmons, M. & Richardson, D. (1981). *The Assertive Christian.* Minneapolis: Winston Press.

Emmons, M. & Alberti, R. (1983). Failure: winning at the losing game in assertiveness training. In Foa, E. & Emmelkamp, P. (eds.) *Failures in Behavior Thearpy.* New York: Wiley, 121-136.

Eriksen, L., Mossige, S. & Johansen, K.G. (1979). Behaviour therapy methods with alcoholics: Assertiveness, self-control and systematic desensitization/relaxation. (Norg) *Scandinavian Journal of Behaviour Therapy, 8* (2), 69-82.

Everhart, Gary & others. (1980). Assertive skills training for the blind. *Journal of Visual Impairment and Blindness, 74,* 62-65.

Faily, et al. (1977). *Leadership Development: Assertive Training for Nurses.* Chapel Hill, North Carolina: School of Nursing. Second Edition 1979.

Fensterheim, H. (1980). A behavioral method for improving sport performance. *Psychiatric Annals, 10,,* 54-63.

Fensterheim, H. (1972). Assertive methods and marital problems. In R. Rubin, H. Fensterheim, J. Henderson, & L. Ullmann (Eds.), *Advances in Behavior Therapy.* New York: Academic Press.

Fensterheim, H. (1971). *Help Without Psychoanalysis.* New York: Stein and Day.

Fensterheim, H. & Bauer, J. (1975). *Don't Say Yes When You Want to Say No.* New York: Dell.

Fiedler, D. & Beach, L.R. (1978). On the decision to be assertive. *Journal of Consulting and Clinical Psychology, 46,* 537-546.

Foxx, R.M. & McMorrow, M.J. (1985). Teaching social skills to mentally retarded adults: Follow-up results from three studies. *The Behavior Therapist 8,* 4, 71-76.

Freedberg, E.J. & Johnston, W.E. (1981). Effects of alcoholism assertion training within context of a multi-modal alcoholism treatment program for employed alcoholics. *Psychological Reports, 48,* 379-386.

Freeman, A., Simon, K., Buetler, L., & Arkowitx, H. (Eds.) (1989). *Comprehensive Handbook of Cognitive Therapy.* New York: Plenum Press.

Freud, S. (1962). *Civilization and Its Discontents.* London: The Hogarth Press, Ltd.

Friedman, P.H. (1971). The effects of modeling and role playing on assertive behavior. In R. Rubin, A. Lazarus, H. Fensterheim, & C. Franks (Eds.), *Advances in Behavior Therapy.* New York: Academic Press.

Futch, E.J., Scheirer, C.J. & Lisman, S.A. (1982). Factor analyzing a scale of assertiveness: A critique and demonstration. *Behavior Modification, 6,* 24-43.

Galassi, J.P., DeLo, J.S., Galassi, M.D., & Bastien, S. (1974). The College Self-Expression Scale: A measure of assertiveness. *Behavior Therapy, 5,* 165-171.

Galassi, J.P. & Galassi, M.D. (1977). Assessment procedures for assertive behavior. In R.E. Alberti (Ed.), *Assertiveness: Innovations, Applications, Issues.* San Luis Obispo, California: Impact Publishers, Inc.

Galassi, M.D. & Galassi, J.P. (1980). Similarities and differences between two assertion measures: Factor analyses of the College Self-expression Scale and the Rathus Assertiveness Schedule. *Behavioral Assessment, 2,* 43-57.

Gambrill, E.D. & Richey, C.A. (1975). An assertion inventory for use in assessment and research. *Behavior Therapy, 6,* 550-561.

Garner, P.A. (1982). Assertiveness not aggression: A management skill for the 80's. *Management, 34,* 28-31.

Gay, J.E. (1982). Assertive discipline: A panacea for the administrator's discipline problems? *Education, 103,* 173-174.

Gay, M.L., Hollandsworth, J.G. Jr., & Galassi, J.P. (1975). An assertiveness inventory for adults. *Journal of Counseling Psychology, 22,* 340-344.

Getter, H. & Nowinski, J.K. (1981). A free response test of interpersonal effectiveness. *Journal of Personality Assessment, 45* (3), 301-308.

Goddard, R.C. (1981). Increase in assertiveness and actualization as a function of didactic training. *Journal of Counseling Psychology, 28* (4), 279-287.

Golden, M. (1981). A measure of cognition within the context of assertion. *Journal of Clinical Psychology, 37,* 253-262.

Goldstein-Fodor, I., & Epstein, R. (1983). Assertiveness training for women: Where are we failing? In Foa, E. & Emmelkamp, P. (eds.) *Failures in Behavior Thearpy.* New York: Wiley, 137-158.

Gordon, S. & Waldo, M. (1984). The effects of assertiveness training on couples' relationships. *American Journal of Family Therapy, 12,* 73-77.

Gorecki, P.R., Dickson, A.L., Anderson, H.N. & Jones, G.E. (1981). Relationship between contrived *in vivo* and role- play assertive behavior. *Journal of Clinical Psychology, 37* (1), 104-107.

Gormally, J. (1982). Evaluation of assertiveness: Effects of gender, rater involvement and level of assertiveness. *Behavior Therapy, 13,* 219-225.

Greenwald, D.P., et al. (1981). Differences between social skills therapists and psychotherapists in treating depression. *Journal of Consulting and Clinical Psychology, 49* (5), 757-759.

Grodner, B.S. (1977). Assertiveness and anxiety: a cross-cultural and socio-economic perspective. In R.E. Alberti (Ed.), *Assertiveness: Innovations, Applications, Issues.* San Luis Obispo, California: Impact Publishers, Inc.

Grunebaum, H. (1979). Middle age and marriage: Affiliative men and assertive women. *American Journal of Family Therapy, 7* (3), 46-50.

Guerra, J.J. & Taylor, P.A. (1977). The four assertive myths: a fable. In R.E. Alberti (Ed.), *Assertiveness: Innovations, Applications, Issues.* San Luis Obispo, California: Impact Publishers, Inc.

Gulanick, N.A. & Howard, G.S. (1979). Evaluation of a group program designed to increase androgyny in feminine women. *Sex Roles, 5,* (6), 811-827.

Hammen, C.L., Jacobs, M., Mayal, A. & Cochran, S.D. (1980). Dysfunctional cognitions and the effectiveness of skills and cognitive-behavioral assertion training. *Journal of Consulting and Clinical Psychology, 48,* 685-695.

Hammond, P.D. & Oei, T.P. (1982). Social skills training and cognitive restructuring with sexual unassertiveness in women. *Journal of Sex and Marital Therapy, 8,* 297-304.

Hart, E.W. (1977). Levels of assertiveness. *Transactional Analysis Journal, 7* (2), 173-165.

Heimberg, R.G. & Becker, R.E. (1981). Cognitive and behavioral models of assertive behavior: Review, analysis, and integration. *Clinical Psychology Review, 1,* 353-373.

Henderson, M. (1983). Self-reported assertion and aggression among violent offenders with high or low levels of overcontrolled hostility. *Personality and Individual Differences, 4,* 113-115.

Herman, S.J. (1977). Assertiveness: One answer to job dissatisfaction for nurses. In R. E. Alberti (Ed.), *Assertiveness: Innovations, Applications, Issues.* San Luis Obispo, California: Impact Publishers, Inc.

Herman, S. (1978). *Becoming Assertive: A Guide for Nurses.* New York: D. Van Nostrand Company.

Hersen, M., Bellack, A.S. & Himmelhoch, J.M. (1980). Treatment of unipolar depression with social skills training. *Behavior Modification, 4* (4), 547-556.

Hestand, R., et al. (1971). The Willoughby schedule: A replication. *Journal of Behavior Therapy and Experimental Psychiatry, 2,* 111-112.

Higgins, R.L., Frisch, M.B. & Smith, D. (1983). A comparison of role-played and natural responses to identical circumstances. *Behavior Therapy, 14,* 158-169.

Hill, D. (1990, April). Order in the classroom. *Teacher Magazine,* 70-77.

Hollandsworth, J.G., Jr. (1985). Social validation of a construct for differentiating assertion and aggression. *The Behavior Therapist, 8,* 7, 136-138.

Hollin, C. & Trower, P. (1988). Development and applications of social skills training: a review and critique. In Hersen, M., Eisler, R., and Miller, P. (eds.), *Progress in Behavior Modification,* 20: 165-214.

Horan, J.J. & Williams, J.M. (1982). Longitudinal study of assertion training as a drug abuse prevention strategy. *American Educational Research Journal, 19,* 341-351.

Houts, P. & Serber, M. (1972). *After The Turn-On, What?* Champaign, Illinois: Research Press.

Howard, G.S., et al. (1980). Is a behavioral measure the best estimate of behavioral parameters? Perhaps not. *Applied Psychological Measurement, 4* (3), 293-311.

Hung, J.H., Rosenthal, T.L. & Kelley, J.E. (1980). Social comparison standards spur immediate assertion: "So you think you're submissive?" *Cognitive Therapy and Research, 4,* 223-234.

Hwang, P.O. (1977). Assertion training for Asian-Americans. In R.E. Alberti (Ed.), *Assertiveness: Innovations, Applications, Issues.* San Luis Obispo, California: Impact Publishers, Inc.

Jacobs, M.K. & Cochran, S.D. (1982). The effects of cognitive restructuring on assertive behavior. *Cognitive Therapy and Research, 6,* 63-76.

Jones, R.G. (1968). *A Factored Measure of Ellis' Irrational Belief Systems with Personality and Maladjustment Correlated.* Wichita, Kansas: Test Systems.

Jones, S.L. (1984). Assertiveness training in Christian perspective. *Journal of Psychology and Theology, 12,* 91- 99.

Jordan, C.S., Davis, M., Kahn, P. & Sinnott, R.H. (1980). Eidetic-imagery group methods of assertion training. *Journal of Mental Imagery, 4,* 41-48.

Joyce, B. & Weil, M. (1986). *Models of Teaching* (3rd edition). Englewood Cliffs, NJ: Prentice-Hall (383-397).

Kaplan, D. (1982). Behavioral, cognitive, and behavioral-cognitive approaches to group assertion training therapy. *Cognitive Therapy and Research, 6,* 301-314.

Kazdin, A. (1982). The separate and combined effects of covert and overt rehearsal in developing assertive behavior. *Behaviour Research and Therapy, 20,* 17-25.

Kazdin, A.E. (1980). Covert and overt rehearsal and elaboration during treatment in the development of assertive behavior. *Behaviour Research & Therapy, 18* (3), 191-201.

Kazdin, A.E. (1978). *History of Behavior Modification.* Baltimore: University Park Press.

Kazdin, A.E. & Mascitelli, S. (1982). Covert and overt rehearsal and homework practice in developing assertiveness. *Journal of Consulting and Clinical Psychology, 50,* 250- 258.

Kazdin, A., & Smith, G. (1979). Covert conditioning: A review and evaluation. *Advanced Behavior Research and Therapy, 2,* 57- 98.

Keane, T.M., Wedding, D. & Kelly, J.A. (1983). Assessing subjective responses to assertive behavior: Data from patient samples. *Behavior Modification, 7,* 317-330.

Keet, R. & Nelson, M. (1986). *Shopper's Guide to the Medical Marketplace.* San Luis Obispo, California: Impact Publishers.

Kelly, J.A. (1985). Group social skills training. *The Behavior Therapist, 8,* 5, 93-95.

Kendall, P.C. & Hollon, S. (Eds.) (1981) *Assessment Strategies for Cognitive-Behavioral Interventions.* New York: Academic Press, 1981.

Kendall, P.C., & Kriss, M.R. (1983). Cognitive-behavioral interventions. In C. E. Walker (Ed.), *Handbook of Clinical Psychology.* Homewood, Ill.: Dow Jones-Irwin.

Kern, J.M. (1982). Predicting the impact of assertive, empathic-assertive, and nonassertive behavior: The assertiveness of the assertee. *Behavior Therapy, 13,* 486-498.

Kern, M. & MacDonald, M.L. (1980). Assessing assertion: An investigation of construct validity and reliability. *Journal of Consulting and Clinical Psychology, 48* (4), 532-534.

Kidder, L.H., Boell, J.L. & Moyer, M.M. (1983). Rights consciousness and victimization prevention: Personal defense and assertiveness training. *Journal of Social Issues, 39(2),* 153-168.

Kiecolt-Gläser, J.K. & Greenberg, B. (1983). On the use of physiological measures in assertion research. *Journal of Behavioral Assessment, 5,* 97-109.

Klass, E.T. (1981). A cognitive analysis of guilt over assertion. *Cognitive Therapy and Research, 5,* 283-297.

Kolotkin, R.A. (1980). Situation specificity in the assessment of assertion: Considerations for the measurement of training and transfer. *Behavior Therapy, 11,* 651-661.

Kuperminc, M. & Heimberg, R.G. (1983). Consequence probability and utility as factors in the decision to behave assertively. *Behavior Therapy, 14,* 637-646.

L'Abate, L. & Milan, M.A. (Eds.) (1985). *Handbook of Social Skills Training and Research.* New York: John Wiley & Sons.

Ladd, G.W. & Mize, J. (1983). A cognitive-social learning model of social-skill learning. *Psychological Review, 90,* 127- 157.

LaGreca, A.M. & Santogrossi, D.A. (1980). Social skills training with elementary school students: A behavioral group approach. *Journal of Consulting and Clinical Psychology, 48* (2), 220- 227.

Landau, P. & Paulson, T. (1977). Group assertion training for Spanish speaking Mexican-American mothers. In R.E. Alberti (Ed.), *Assertiveness: Innovations, Applications, Issues.* San Luis Obispo, California: Impact Publishers, Inc.

Lang, P. (1984). *Cognitive and physiological linkage: Implications for behavior therapy.* Invited Address presented at the 18th Annual Convention of the Association for Advancement of Behavior Therapy, Philadelphia, PA.

Lange, A.J. & Jakubowski, P. (1976). *The Assertive Option.* Champaign: Research Press.

Lawrence, P.S. (1970). The assessment and modification of assertive behavior. Doctoral dissertation, Arizona State University. *Dissertation Abstracts International, 31,* lB- 1601B and University Microfilms No. 70-11, 888.

Lawson, L.G., Donant, F.D., & Lawson, J.D. (1982). *Lead On! The Complete Handbook for Group Leaders.* San Luis Obispo, CA: Impact Publishers, Inc.

Lazarus, A.A. (1971). *Behavior Therapy and Beyond.* New York: McGraw-Hill.

Lazarus, A.A. (Ed.) (1972). *Clinical Behavior Therapy.* New York: Brunner/Mazel.

Lazarus, A.A. (1985). *Marital Myths.* San Luis Obispo, California: Impact Publishers.

Lazarus, A. (1976). *Multimodal Behavior Therapy.* New York: Springer.

Leah, J.A., Law, H.G. & Snyder, C.W. (1979). The structure of self-reported difficulty in assertiveness: An application of three-mode common factor analysis. *Multivariate Behavioral Research,* 14, 443-462.

Lefevre, E.R. & West, M. (1984). Expressed Priorities of Assertiveness Trainees. *Canadian Counsellor, 18,* 168-173.

Lehman-Olson, D. (1978). Assertiveness training: Theoretical and clinical implications, In Olson, D.H. (ed.) *Treating Relationships,* Lake Mills, IA: Graphic Publishing.93-116.

Liberman, R.P., King, L.W., DeRisi, W.J., & McCann, M. (1976). *Personal Effectiveness.* Champaign, Illinois: Research Press.

Lineburger, M.H. & Calhoun, K.S. (1983). Assertive behavior in black and white American undergraduates. *Journal of Psychology, 113,* 139-148.

Linehan, M.M., Goldfried, M.R. & Goldfried, A.P. (1979). Assertion therapy: Skill training or cognitive restructuring. *Behavior Therapy, 10,* 372-388.

Lorenz, K. (1966) *On Aggression.* New York: Harcourt, Brace and World.

Lorr, M., More, W.W. & Mansueto, S. (1981). The structure of assertiveness: A confirmatory study. *Behaviour Research & Therapy, 19* (2), 153-156.

MacNeilage, L.A. & Adams, K.A. (1982). *Assertiveness at Work.* Englewood Cliffs, NJ: Prentice Hall.

MacNeilage, L.A. & Adams, K.A. (1977). The method of contrasted role-plays: An insight-oriented model for role playing in assertiveness training groups. Paper presented at the American Psychological Association.

Mahoney, M.J. (1974). *Cognition and Behavior Modification.* Cambridge, Mass.: Ballinger.

Marshall, P.G., et al. (1981). Anxiety reduction, assertive training, and enactment of consequences. *Behavior Modification, 5* (1), 85-102.

Martin, C.V. (1980). Social skill development in delinquent adolescent patients. *Corrective and Social Psychiatry and Journal of Behavior Technology, Methods and Therapy, 26,* 35-36.

Mauger, P., et al. (1980). *Interpersonal Behavior Survey.* Los Angeles: Western Psychological Service.

McAllister, E.W. (1975). Assertive training and the Christian therapist. *Journal of Psychology and Theology,* Winter, 19-24.

McCarthy, D. & Bellucci, J. (1974). The adolescent self-expression scale. Personal communication.

McCormack, S. (1989, Mar.). Response to Render, Padilla and Krank: But educators say it works! *Educational Leadership,* 46 (6): 77-79.

McFall, R.M. & Lillesand, D.B. (1971). Behavior rehearsal with modeling and coaching in assertive training. *Journal of Abnormal Psychology, 77* (3), 313-323.

McFall, R.M. & Marston, A.R. (1970). An experimental investigation of behavior rehearsal in assertiveness training. *Journal of Abnormal Psychology, 76,* 295-303.

McFall, R.M. & Twentyman, C.T. (1973). Four experiments on the relative contributions of rehearsal, modeling, and coaching to assertion training. *Journal of Abnormal Psychology, 81,* 199-218.

McKay, M., Rogers, P, & McKay, J. (1989). *When Anger Hurts.* Berkeley, CA: New Harbinger Publications.

Meichenbaum, D. *Cognitive-Behavior Modification: An Integrative Approach.* New York: Plenum, 1977.

Merluzzi, T., Glass, C. & Genest, M. (Eds.) *Cognitive Assessment.* New York: Guilford, 1981.

Michelson, Larry & Wood, Randy (1980). A group assertive training program for elementary schoolchildren. *Child Behavior Therapy, 2,* 1-9.

Miller, T.W.(1982). Assertiveness training for coaches: The issue of healthy communication between coaches and players. *Journal of Sport Psychology, 4,* 107-114.

Montgomery, D. & Heimberg, R.G. (1978). Assertiveness training: Overcoming obstacles to change. *Professional Psychology, 9,* 220-227.

Moy, A.C. (1980). Assertive behavior in a new testament perspective. *Journal of Psychology and Theology, 8,* 288-292.

Muehlenhard, C.L. & McFall, R.M. (1983). Automated assertion training: A feasibility study. *Journal of Social and Clinical Psychology, 1(3),* 246-258.

Ness, M.K., Donnan, H.H. & Jenkins, J. (1983). Race as an interpersonal variable in negative assertion. *Journal of Clinical Psychology, 39,* 361-369.

Otto, H. (1969). *More Joy in Your Marriage.* New York: Hawthorn Books, Inc.

Palmer, P. (1977). *Liking Myself.* San Luis Obispo, California: Impact Publishers, Inc.

Palmer, P. (1977). *The Mouse, the Monster, and Me: Assertiveness for Young People.* San Luis Obispo, California: Impact Publishers, Inc.

Pearson, J.C. (1979). A factor analytic study of the items in the Rathus assertiveness schedule and the personal report of communication apprehension. *Psychological Reports, 45 (2),* 491-497.

Perkins, R.J. & Kemmerling, R.G. (1983). Effect of para-professional-led assertiveness training on levels of assertiveness and self-actualization. *Journal of College Student Personnel, 21,* 61-66.

Perls, F.S. (1969). *Gestalt Therapy Verbatim.* Lafayette, California: Real People Press.

Peters, T., & Austin, N. (1985). *A Passion for Excellence.* New York: Random House.

Phelps, S. & Austin, N. (1975, 1987). *The Assertive Woman.* San Luis Obispo, California: Impact Publishers, Inc.

Piercy, F.P. (1980). Birth of a person: One woman's reflections on survival and growth. *Personnel and Guidance Journal, 59,* 74-78.

Pinhas, V. (1980). Sex guilt and sexual control in women alcoholics in early sobriety. *Sexuality and Disability, 3,* 256-272.

Pitcher, S.W. & Meikle, S. (1980). The topography of assertive behavior in positive and negative situations. *Behavior Therapy, 11,* 532-547.

Queiroz, L.O. et.al. (1981). A functional analysis of obsessive-compulsive problems with related therapeutic procedures. *Behaviour Research and Therapy, 19,* 377-388.

Rathus, S.A. (1973). A 30-item schedule for assessing assertive behavior. *Behavior Therapy, 4,* 398-406.

Rathus, S.A. & Nivid, J.S. (1978). *BT: Behavior Therapy.* New York: Doubleday.

Reath, R.A., Piercy, F., Hovestadt, A. & Oliver, M. (1980). Assertion and marital adjustment. *Family Relations, 29,* 249-253.

Render, G. (1989, Mar.). What research really shows about assertive discipline. *Educational Leadership,* 46 (6): 72- 75.

Replogle, W., O'Bannonn, R., McCullough, P. & Cashion, L. (1980). Locus of control and assertive behavior. *Psychological Reports, 47,* 769-770.

Rich, A.R. & Schroeder, H.E. (1976). Research issues in assertiveness training. *Psychological Bulletin, 83,* 6, 1081-1096.

Riddle, P. & Johnson, G.A. (1983). Sexual harassment: What role should health educators play? *Health Education, 14,* 20-23.

Rimm, D.C., Hill, G.A., Brown, N.N., and Stuart, J.E. (1974). Group assertive training in the treatment of inappropriate anger expression. *Psychological Reports, 34,* 791-798.

Rimm, D.C., et al. (1976). Assertive training versus rehearsal, and the importance of making an assertive response. *Behaviour Research and Therapy. 14,* 315-321.

Rippere, V. (1983). Nutritional approaches to behavior modification. In M. Hersen, R. Eisler, P. Miller (Eds.), *Progress In Behavior Modification.* New York: Academic Press, *14.*

Rogers, C.R. (1961). *On Becoming a Person.* Boston: Houghton-Mifflin.

Rose, S.D., Tolman, R. & Tallant, S. (1985). Group process in cognitive-behavioral therapy. *The Behavior Therapist, 8,* 4, 77-78.

Rose, Y.J. & Tryon, W.W. (1979). Judgments of assertive behavior as a function of speech loudness, latency, content, gestures, inflection, and sex. *Behavior Modification, 3,* 112-123.

Rosenbaum, A. & Oleary, K. D. (1981). Marital violence: Characteristics of abusive couples. *Journal of Consulting and Clinical Psychology, 49,* 63-71.

Rosenthal, T. & Reese, S. (1976). The effects of covert and overt modeling on assertive behavior. *Behaviour Research and Therapy, 14,* 463-469.

Rotter, J.B. (1966). Generalized expectancies for internal versus external control of reinforcement. *Psychological Monographs, 80,* 1-28.

Ruben, D.H. (1983). Methodological adaptations in assertiveness training programs designed for the blind. *Psychological Reports, 53,* 1281-1282.

Ruben, D.H. (1985). *Progress in Assertiveness, 1973-1983: An Analytical Bibliography.* Metuchen, N.J.: The Scarecrow Press, Inc.

Ruben, D.H. & Ruben, M. (1989, Aug.). Why assertiveness training programs fail. *Small Group Behavior,* 20 (3): 367-380.

Rush, A.J., Shaw, B.F., & Khatami, M. (1980). Cognitive therapy of depression: Utilizing the couples system. *Cognitive Research and Therapy, 4,* 103-113.

Russell, R.A. (1983). Cognitive barriers to assertiveness for the Christian. *Counseling and Values, 27,* 83-89.

Russell, R.A. (1981). Assertiveness training and its effects upon the marital relationship. *Family Therapy, 8,* 9-20.

Sacherman, C. (1979). Using the Gambrill-Richey assertion inventory to personalize assertion training. *Journal for Specialists in Group Work,* (4) 1.

Safran, J.D., Alden, L.E. & Davidson, P.O. (1980). Client anxiety level as a moderator variable in assertion training. *Cognitive Therapy and Research, 4,* 189-200.

Salter, A. (1949, 1961). *Conditioned Reflex Therapy.* New York: Farrar, Straus, and Giroux (1949); Capricorn Books edition (1961).

Sanchez, V. & Lewinsohn, P.M. (1980). Assertive behavior and depression. *Journal of Consulting and Clinical Psychology, 48* (1), 119-120.

Sanders, R. (1976). The effectiveness of a theologically oriented approach to assertive training for refusal behaviors. Masters Thesis. S.F. Austin State University, *Masters abstracts, 14,* 252. (University Microfilm No. 13-08786).

Sanders, R. & Malony, H.N. (1982). A theological and psychological rationale for assertiveness training. *Journal of Psychology and Theology, 10,* 251-255.

Schwartz, R.M. & Gottman, I.M. (1976). Toward a task analysis of assertive behavior. *Journal of Consulting and Clinical Psychology, 44,* 910-920.

Seligman, M.E. (1973). Fall into helplessness. *Psychology Today,* June, 43.

Serber, M. (1971). Teaching the non-verbal components of assertive training. *Journal of Behavior Therapy and Experimental Psychiatry, 3,* 1-5.

Shaffer, C.S., Shapiro, J., Sank, L.I. & Coghlan, J. (1981). Positive changes in depression, anxiety, and assertion following individual and group cognitive behavior therapy intervention. *Cognitive Therapy & Research, 5* (2).

Shaw, M. (1979). *Assertive-Responsive Management.* Reading, Mass.: Addison-Wesley.

Sheehy, G. (1976). *Passages: Predictable Crises of Adult Life.* New York: E.P. Dutton and Company.

Shelton, J. & Ackerman, M. (1974). *Homework in Counseling and Psychotherapy: Examples of Systematic Assignments for Therapeutic Use by Mental Health Professionals.* Springfield, Illinois: Charles C. Thomas.

Smaby, M.H. & Tamminen, A.W. (1976). Counselors can be assertive. *Personnel and Guidance Journal, 54,* 420-424.

Snyder, G.R. (1982). A consideration of Christ's aggressive behavior within a global model of assertiveness. *Journal of Psychology and Christianity, 1,* 39-44.

Stefanek, M. & Eisler, R. (1983). The current status of cognitive variables in assertiveness training. *Progress in Behavior Modification,* 15: 277-319.

St. Lawrence, J. (1987). Assessment of assertion. In Hersen, M., Eisler, R., and Miller, P. (eds.), *Progress in Behavior Modification,* 21: 152-190.

Stringer-Moore, D. & Jack, G. (1977, 1979, 1981, 1983).*Assertive Behavior Training: An Annotated Bibliography.* San Luis Obispo, California: Impact Publishers, Inc.

Suinn, R. (1985). Imagery rehearsal applications to performance enhancement. *The Behavior Therapist, 8,* 155-159.

Tamminen, A.W. & Smaby, M.H. (1981). Helping counselors learn to confront. *Personnel and Guidance Journal, 60,* 41-45.

Tanabe-Endsley, P. (1974, 1979). *Project Write.* El Cerrito, CA: Author. (1421 Arlington, 94530).

Tavris, C., (1982). *Anger: The Misunderstood Emotion.* New York: Simon & Schuster.

Taylor, J.A. (1953). A personality scale of manifest anxiety. *Journal of Abnormal and Social Psychology, 48,* 285-290.

Thurman, C.W. (1985). Effectiveness of cognitive-behavioral treatments in reducing Type A behavior among university faculty. *Journal of Counseling Psychology, 32,* 74-83.

Trower, P. (1980a). How to lose friends and influence nobody: An analysis of social failure. In W. Singleton et al. (Eds.), *The Analysis of Social Skills.* New York: Plenum Press.

Trower, P. (1980). Situational analysis of the components and processes of behavior of socially skilled and unskilled patients. *Journal of Consulting and Clinical Psychology, 48* (3), 327-339.

Tucker, R.K., Weaver, R.L., Duran, R.L. & Redden, E.M. (1983). Criterion-related validity of three measures of assertiveness. *Psychological Reports, 33,* 361-370.

Tucker, R.K., Weaver, R.L. & Redden, E.M. (1983). Differentiating assertiveness, aggressiveness, and shyness: A factor analysis. *Psychological Reports, 53,* 607-611.

Turner, R.M., Ditomasso, R.A. & Murray, M.R. (1980). Psychometric analysis of the Willoughby Personality Schedule. *Journal of Behavior Therapy and Experimental Psychiatry, 11,* 185-194.

Twentyman, C.T., Gibralter, J.C. & Inz, J.M. (1979). Multimodal assessment of rehearsal treatments in an assertion training program. *Journal of Counseling Psychology, 26,* 383-389.

Twentyman, C., Pharr, D.R. & Connor, J.M. (1980). A comparison of three covert assertion training procedures. *Journal of Clinical Psychology, 36,* 520-525.

Ulene, A. (1977). *Feeling Fine.* New York: St. Martin's Press.

Vaal, J.J., McCullagh, J. (1975). The Rathus assertiveness schedule: Reliability at the junior high school level. *Behavior Therapy, 6,* 566-567.

Vagg, P. (Ed.). (1979). Assessment in assertiveness training. *ASSERT: The Newsletter of Assertive Behavior, 28,* 1, 3.

Van Erven, T. (1980). Assertiveness: A review. *Tijdschrift Voor Psychotherapie, 6,* 33-43.

Warehime, R.G. & Lowe, D.R. (1983). Assessing assertiveness in work settings: A discrimination measure. *Psychological Reports, 53,* 1007-1012.

Watson, D.W., & Friend, R. (1969). Measurement of social-evaluative anxiety. *Journal of Consulting and Clinical Psychology,* 33: 448-457.

Watson, D.W. & Maisto, S.A. (1983). A review of the effectiveness of assertiveness training in the treatment of alcohol abusers. *Behavioural Psychotherapy, 11,* 36-49.

Westefeld, J.S., Galassi, J., Galassi, M. (1980). Effects of role-playing instructions on assertive behavior: A methodological study. *Behavior Therapy, 11* (2), 271-277.

Wilson, G.T. & O'Leary, K.D. (1980). *Principles of behavior therapy.* Englewood Cliffs, N.J.: Prentice Hall.

Wolfe, J. & Fodor, I. (1975). A cognitive/behavioral approach to modifying assertive behavior in women. *The Counseling Psychologist, 5* (4), 45-52.

Wollman, N. (Ed.) (1985). *Working for Peace: A Handbook of Practical Psychology And Other Tools.* San Luis Obispo, California: Impact Publishers.

Wolpe, J. (1958). *Psychotherapy by Reciprocal Inhibition.* Stanford: Stanford University Press.

Wolpe, J. (1969, 1973). *The Practice of Behavior Therapy.* New York: Pergamon Press.

Wolpe, J. & Lang, P. (1964). A fear survey schedule for use in behavior therapy. *Behavior Research and Therapy, 2,* 27- 30.

Wolpe, J. & Lazarus, A.A. (1966). *Behavior Therapy Techniques.* New York: Pergamon Press, (out of print).

Yalom, I.D. (1970, 1975, 1985). *The Theory and Practice of Group Psychotherapy.* New York: Basic Books.

Yanagida, E.H. (1979). Cross cultural considerations in the application of assertion training: A brief note. *Pychology of Women Quarterly, 3* (4), 400-402.

INDEX